The Tyne

David Bean

ISBN 1 901237 29 X

Published by TUPS Books, 38 Hutton Close,
Crowther Industrial Estate, Washington,
Tyne and Wear, NE38 0AH
Tel: 0191 419 0446 Fax: 0191 419 2647

Introduction

I was once gently but firmly rebuked by a devotee of the waters of Tweed for referring to her river as '*The* Tweed'. One did not use the definite article, she explained: the correct name was, simply, 'Tweed'. Thankyou, ma'am: we learn something every day. But — Tweed is a river that lives on money and sport. The Tyne has always worked hard for its living and so needs no affectation of title — it's always been simply 'The Tyne'.

It is a river famous all over the world. To most people it's known best for its industrial traditions—for its coal, its shipbuilding and engineering—and for its lively, individualistic people. It is seen usually as an urban river which gave over the centuries its inventive genius to the world and more wealth than it was ever able to keep for itself.

In fact most of the Tyne is a country river, draining hundreds of square miles of much of England's greatest visual splendour, vast, lonely tracts which for all their isolation are full of historical as well as scenic interest.

It's three rivers really. North Tyne flows down nearly forty miles from the Scottish Border to meet its twin South Tyne, of a similar length, near Hexham, on its way from the highest Pennines. Then united they flow on for another forty miles through mostly rolling countryside on their way to the North Sea. Only the Tyne's final dozen miles are truly urban. The rest is mostly sheer beauty.

There really should be no such thing as an ideal time to produce a guide book. Things change. No sooner does a writer wax lyrical about a view than some clown spoils it all by building a housing estate across it. No sooner does he praise the industry of workers in a town than the backside falls out of it and their factory is closed down. The Tyne is a different river now than when I set out to write about it just a few months ago; it will be different again when these words are read. If.

And yet the turn of the Millennium is as good a time to write about such things as any. Great changes are happening for the good as well as for the bad—or these days, too often, the mediocre. While work in the towns is diminishing, access to the countryside has never been easier since the days when our ancestors roamed across it wearing little more than coats of blue paint. Not only is a Right to Roam a distinct possibility, but hundreds of miles of footpaths and cycle ways are in the process of being opened up.

SUSTRANS (Sustainable Transport) is opening 5,000 miles of its National Cycle Network. An important section of this continuous way follows the areas described in this book. At the same time the Countryside Agency is establishing a bridleway right up the Pennines, again covering much of the territory described here, particularly that within reach of both North and South Tyne.

In addition there are more opportunities than ever before to learn about the older ways of life in these areas. For example, knowledge of and interest in the long tradition of lead and silver production, particularly above the South Tyne, all but faded out. Now the visitor is spoiled for choice of heritage sites where everything he might want to know about the industry is at hand. All, that is, except the industry itself.

On top of all this a new spirit of pride has taken over the towns at the mouth of the river. Newcastle itself, never dull, is now one of the liveliest cities in Britain, while neighbouring Gateshead has at last pulled itself up by its own efforts into an international cultural and sporting centre.

While it is not yet much more than a dream to expect public transport to link all the wonderful spots in the region of the triple Tynes, yet I would join with SUSTRANS in urging people to use what there is and to leave cars behind. They will see a lot more on foot or by push-bike—quality if not quantity.

Contents

Part 1 — The South Tyne

Part Two — The North Tyne

Part Three — The Combine Tynes

David Bean: Although born in London before the war, David Bean has lived and worked on or near the Tyne for much of the past half century. He has published a dozen books, both fiction and non-fiction, most of them set in the north. *Bean's Boots* (BBC) and *The Hopeful Traveller* (ITV) covered the area on film.

Photographs:

Ken Rowley: Pages 15, 16, 20, 21, 25, 28, 30. 37, 38, 39, 40, 42, 43, 46, 48, 50, 51, 52, 54, 61, 63, 64, 65, 68, 71, 73, 81, 83, 85, 87, 88, 89, 91, 92, 94, 95, 97,99, 100, 101 103 104, 105, 106, 107, 108, 111, 112, 123, 124, 125, 126, 127, 128, 130, 131, 132, 133, 134, 135, 136, 137, 138, 139, 140, 141, 142, 143, 144, 145, 147, 148, 149, 150, 151, 152, 153, 155, 156, 157, 158, 159, 160, 161, 162, 163, 164, 165, 166, 167,

Michael Swan: Pages, 1, 2, 3, 4, 5, 9, 10, 11, 12, 14, 17, 19, 22, 23, 24, 26, 29, 31, 32, 33, 34, 35

Ken Rowley was born on the banks of the Tyne in 1951, in Tyne Terrace, North Shields. He learned most of his photography skills at North Shields People's Centre. He completed a BA Honours Degree in Contemporary Photography Practises at Northumbria University, Newcastle, in 1998 and now teaches photography skills at North Shields Town Training Centre.

Michael Swan heads a walking tour company operating largely in the vicinity Hadrian's Wall and the Tyne Valley

Part One — The South Tyne

Chapter One

Source to Alston

*Until 2001 there was nothing to mark the source,
now it has a sculpture all of its own*

Peace, calm, stillness, a silence broken only by the sighing of the wind and the rippling trickle of fast-running burns. The smell of the peat — twelve feet deep here in places. It's the loneliest place in all England. It's all as if man had never touched it — at first sight.

The River South Tyne rises in Cumbria under Cross Fell, highest point in all the Pennine Chain. England's last wilderness, David Bellamy has called it, and great country for the rising of the waters. For not only Tyne is born here: just a few miles away these hills have been midwife to the River Tees, running parallel with it to the North Sea, likewise the Wear on its way to Sunderland, and to feeders of the River Eden to the west, bound for the Irish Sea.

The source of the South Tyne itself is hardly dramatic There's only a sculpture, or hewn stone, to mark it, and that put up only in 2001. There is no sudden gushing from the wild fell, just a number of little burns, hardly showing above the tussocks in summer, and even when they join together they run only a foot or two wide, fast and burbling through the bents and heather, splashing from time to time over sills of the underlying rock.

To reach this spot you must walk, thank God, or there would be no wilderness left any more. The nearest road-head, and that a narrow one, is over two miles away to the north, and there is no driveable access the other way. There is a jeepable track (as the French say) which follows the young river, but it leads only to Moor House, focus of the largest nature reserve in England, a Biosphere Reserve of great scientific importance, managed by English Nature.

South Tyne Source — now you see it, now you don't

2

Moor House was once reckoned to be the loneliest inhabited settlement in England. It had been a shooting-box, and for a while after the shooting was banned there was a permanent staff on the spot, studying the unique wild-life. But a succession of rough winters forced them out as far as any continuous residence was concerned.

In 1963 for instance, they were cut off by drifts for over three months, accessible even then only by tough cart-horse. Today the staff make working visits, but because of the nature of their work, and not just the danger of foul weather. Special permission is needed for the public to visit. Contact the Site Manager, English Nature, 01833-622374.

I said earlier that this area looks as if man had never touched it. This is clearly not the case if you lift up the eyes to the Pennine tops and find the great white golf-ball and radar masts on top of Great Dun Fell. You can see it from miles away in any direction, and not only would it be

a saving landmark for lost walkers, except in a proper white-out, but it is a vital link in the international air-safety network.

But there's more of man's activity about this area than so easily meets the eye. The surface looks poor enough, barely supporting a few sheep, semi-wild. But below there are vast hoards of potential wealth. At least, that's how previous generations saw it. Beneath the peat-clothed rock there is a great reserve of minerals which man counted as riches for hundreds of years, if only he could get to it. Silver's there, zinc, copper, iron, even gold they reckon. And lead. Especially lead.

You don't need to look very far round here to realise that this whole area was once a very busy place indeed, where generations of men, hundreds of them, dug away in the dark looking for the ore which might make them rich, which, smelted and refined, would roof the great cathedrals and palaces of the Middle Ages, and

Great Dun Fell with its golf ball. Cross Fell to the right — highest of all the Pennines

Beneath the trickles great mineral reserves, if you're lucky and dig hard enough

later on produce enough ammunition to wipe out whole generations.

At the height of the lead-mining boom a couple of hundred years ago, this land around the rising of the South Tyne was honeycombed with lead mines. It was like the American Gold Rush almost—a great gamble. Some miners struck it rich, most scratched barely a living. The industry died out earlier last century, but still all around if you look you can see the remains—old waste-heaps on the fell-side which refuse to grow over, hundreds of shafts more or less decayed and some downright dangerous in spite of an

First bridge on the Tyne — another fifty miles to reach the famous giants

Mine shop ruin — weekday home for old-time miners

intensive effort in recent years to locate old workings and cap off the holes that lead down no-one knows where any more. A saucer-shaped depression in the ground, although apparently grassed over, can still open up under the feet of the unwary like an Alpine crevasse, so it is best to keep it at a respectful distance.

Lead is widely believed to have been discovered and first worked by the Romans, although there is little enough real evidence on the ground. By

Ashgill Force. South Tyne gets its first big tributary

the old settlement of Tynehead some say that they can still trace the outline of a minor Roman camp on a shelf by the riverside, and that the early conquerors used to dredge pebbles of galena, the ore from which lead is smelted, and not only lead but silver too. If so, no-one has yet found traces of a smelter.

The Romans certainly had the technology: they had picked it up earlier in Spain, and it may be that they passed on their knowledge to the Britons when they left. Certainly both lead and silver were mined here in the Middle Ages— enough silver to make worthwhile the establishment of a Royal Mint at Carlisle and to export the baser metals by pack-mules over fell tracks down to the navigable Tyne and thence out to the rest of the land.

Under the hill of Noonstones (what a magnificent name, although it may be derived from the more prosaic 'Nunstones') ran a mineral vein which was particularly rich in copper. The Great Sulphur Vein was 300 yards wide in one part, and the old miners called it 'The Backbone of the Earth'. Not the backbone of the Tyne, you'll notice, not of just England, but of the whole earth. They were proud men, these old gambling miners, with a great conceit of their worth.

Another visible relic of the old times is what's left of the little stone-built shanties known as 'mine-shops'. Because of the remoteness of most ore-workings, miners' families tended to live in villages further down the valley, but because they were forever looking for new possibilities, sometimes miles away from their base, they would stay for the working week in such

primitive accommodation, walking home for the weekend and back out again the following Monday. These lodgings were cramped and insanitary. Men sometimes slept two or three to a bunk, and they stuffed the ventilation holes to keep out the cold in the hard winters. One inspector in the nineteenth century wrote that the atmosphere in these places was often so bad that he would rather spend 24 hours underground than a quarter-hour in a lodging shop. "I would be terrified," he said.

Not that these lodging miners were anything but peaceable: they would have been too tired to have had time for anything much more than a game of cards (or more likely draughts or chess, for they were most of them serious, deeply religious men), and they sometimes hired an old man to do what cooking they could afford and generally keep the place a bit tidy.

About six miles north of the source of the South Tyne, by which time the riverside road has become metalled, lies the village of Garrigill, once of course a lead-mining settlement but now a generally residential village with a fair trade in the hardier type of summer visitors, especially since the C2C (Sea-to-Sea, geddit?) Cycle Route was established. It is a pleasant enough spot to look at, but nowhere near the busy working place it once was.

In the 1831 census the population was 1,614; by 1970 it had dropped to 135. There were once no fewer than five chapels, all non-conformist of course, and great rivals with each other, and one church. Today the church is still going (if only just) but Garrigill is down to one chapel only.

That and a pub, the George and Dragon, which had a bunk-house attached for cyclists and walkers.

These pedestrians are somewhat different from the old miners tramping to and from their lodging-shops. Most of them, bright in new gear, have just completed, or are about to tackle, the longest, bleakest part of the Pennine Way—the track which leads west to the top of Cross Fell, highest point in the Pennines.

There's something of a mystery about this track (eight miles to the summit). It's still called the Corpse Path by some of the older locals, and it is supposed to have been used to carry the last mortal remains of Garrigill folk over the shoulder of the height and down another five miles or so to Kirkland in the Eden Valley.

Nothing so very unusual in such an arrangement: burial parties often had to trudge long distances to see that their dear departed were buried in consecrated ground. But there seems to be no record of any Garrigill names in the Kirkland registers. None in Alston either, and that's nearer. Perhaps Garrigill folk were like old soldiers, and only faded away.

It may seem a little backside-foremost to kick off a description of a river valley with so much about hills. But one wouldn't be there without the other and Cross Fell seems to have had something which made men eulogise more about it than about other hills twice its size. But then, as the *Gentleman's Magazine* of 1747 said:

> "A mountain that is generally ten months buried in snow and eleven in clouds cannot fail of exciting the attention and curiosity of the traveller."

The *Gentleman's Magazine* exaggerated somewhat. Although Cross Fell is just short of 3,000 feet high and has been known to draw the odd snowflake as late as June and often has a north-facing gully still full of the stuff well into summer, it is usually clear by April. As to cloud, well, it does draw it, but then so do most of the Lake District hills you can see so well from its top. Or would be able to if it wasn't for that cloud.

It must have been clear when a Victorian traveller, quoted by Thomas Sopwith, the celebrated agent of the Blackett-Beaumont mines in Allendale, went to the top and stayed all the summer night to see the sun rise. At three in the morning:

> "a long and thin dark cloud, which stretched along the horizon, suddenly became a brilliant line of refulgent light, a beautiful harbinger of the scarcely more brilliant sun which soon rose with inexpressible grandeur amid the silence and sublimity of the vast scene before us. All nature seemed to respond the deep and solemn feeling impressed by so sublime a spectacle; 'the wilderness and solitary place' again became glad, and the desert seemed once more to rejoice in the commencement of another day."

They don't write travel books like that these days.

Chapter Two

Alston Moor — above ground and below

Nenthead nestling below Dowgang Hush

People still bivouac out on top of Cross Fell in high summer. They can see right down the Pennines, right over the Lakeland mountains, up to the Northumbrian Cheviots and further into Scotland.

There's plenty of room. I've never been able to work out what an acre looks like, but you could, I would guess, mark out four good-sized football pitches on the summit and still have plenty of room for supporters. In 1832, celebrating the passing of the Reform Bill, a huge crowd gathered with fifty brass bands in support. What condition they were in to blow when they had staggered to the top is not recorded.

The Pennine Way and the River South Tyne (now gathering strength and width by the mile) continue northwards to Alston, once capital of the lead-mining area of Alston Moor. It's a pleasant walk, through meadows and woodland, a welcome change no doubt for those who have just braved the bare heights of the Pennine tops. But an interesting diversion is to go from Garrigill up over the hill to its twin village of Nenthead, nearly four miles away along the steep road by the side of Dowgang Hush.

Dowgang is now a local beauty spot, well-wooded, but it should not be forgotten that a 'hush' was another lead-mining term — an artificial gully, or ravine almost here. Caused by lead prospectors damming water and then letting it go suddenly to scour away the surface and expose any mineral veins beneath. It was an early form of opencasting and often quite effective.

Nenthead Reading Room, Britain's first free library.
The old miners were said to prefer books to beer

Dowgang Hush is here because Nenthead was the centre of all the mining activities hereabouts in the nineteenth century — the capital of lead mining, the most important lead town in the country, and probably the world.

Whereas old villages like Garrigill had lead-working imposed upon them — industry growing out of an earlier, purely agricultural way of life, Nenthead was a planned industrial community. It lies in the hollow between Flinty Fell, Middle Fell, and the long, swelling mass of Killhope, which is the watershed over to and

Miners' cottages at Overwater, Nenthead

Earls of Derwentwater after they had been beheaded for their parts in the Jacobite Risings of 1715 and '45. The Quakers made a go of it.

They were progressive not only in their methods of work, but in their attitude towards their work-force. They built sound houses for their miners and smelt-workers, encouraged religion, founded a school which provided the first compulsory education in the land, and a reading-room which housed Britain's first free library.

They forbade swearing and poaching, and discouraged drinking. Before they arrived Nenthead had four pubs; the Quakers got it down to two, and it is recorded that the rent of the Miners' Arms (still there today) had on more than one occasion to be reduced through falling custom; the miners, it was said, preferring books to strong drink.

Benevolent despots, the Quaker Company, with the good sense to see that they could make more money by treating their workers humanely. Farmers had known that of their beasts (if not their labourers) for generations. But they paid about half the rate their men would have got if they had shifted to the expanding coal mines of Durham and Tyneside, and although a reasonable old age pension started at age 65, the average lead miner in the nineteenth century died at 47,

the boundary between Cumbria and County Durham. Lead was mined all about, but Nenthead was the obvious place for a gathering centre, where the galena could be collected and smelted, and so it became under the direction of the London Lead Company, better known locally as the Quaker Company.

They took over an existing smelt mill built in 1738 by a Colonel Liddell who had great expectations of a mine at Rampgill hard by, which never materialised for him. The Quakers had formed their company thirty years earlier, and leased the area around Alston Moor from the Greenwich Hospital for Seamen which in turn had been given the land forfeited by the

Lead mining heritage centre at Nenthead. Once a huge smelter, now a museum

so not many collected. What a stroke of accountancy brilliance!

The Quakers provided land on which their people could establish smallholdings, thus being not only able to feed themselves to a certain extent, but to compensate somewhat for the closed unhealthiness of the mine by what the bosses at least saw as healthy outdoor activity. Poaching being out, cabbage-rearing would have to do as an alternative.

At the height of the London Lead Company's prosperity, the population of Nenthead was over 2,000. Today it is around only a quarter of that. The mining of lead, like all minerals, was subject to frequent fluctuations of the market. The Quaker Company kept going for nearly 200 years, and index-linked its workers' wages to the price of grain. But in late Victorian times things grew so slack that hundreds of miners and their families cleared out — some into the coal industry (always ready to employ strike-breakers against their own more militant workers), while others emigrated to Australia and the New World.

In 1896, however, what looked like good fortune smiled once more. A Belgian company, the Vieille Montaigne Zinc, acquired the local mineral rights and built a huge five-storey, state-of-the-art smelter slap in the middle of the village. They imported Italian miners — the world's best then at overhead rock-drilling — and for a while things went well with the 'Villy Montain', as the old locals still call it. But in 1921 ore output fell alarmingly, and though things went on for a few more years, the plant

being used to extract from the spoil heaps bits of ore former processes had missed, it closed in 1925. Presumably by then the Italians had gone home, though it might make you wonder if they left traces behind them: are there still eyes darker and hair blacker than is usual in the fair-haired North Pennines?

For many years then the place decayed. The heaps refused to grow over, but the buildings crumbled, much of the fine old stone-work of the smelt-mill disappeared in the boots of strangers' cars to build suburban rockeries, and few people except scholars and the occasional ever-optimistic prospector took much notice of the place and its unique history.

In recent years however, there has been a belated surge of interest. The village has been tidied, and the huge smelter site and some of the entrances to the mines themselves have been carefully restored by the North Pennines Heritage Trust. It's an ongoing restoration programme—the smelt mill site and the crushing floor, the barracks where the Italians were housed, the assay house, are all open to the public, and it is planned to open up one or two of the workings themselves. In other words it's another Heritage Centre in a land of heritage centres, and it costs £2 to get in at the time of writing; children etc. less. The Rampgill Cafe is open, or you can picnic, but keep your dogs off the sheep.

There is another visitor centre over the hill at Killhope, with its huge and unique iron water-wheel which used to power all the operations round about. Youngsters can experiment with bits of the old plant, and there's a bit of underground too, to be conducted through, with life-sized waxworks (they'll be plastic today no doubt) of earnest-looking miners doing what earnest-looking miners had to do way back. It's run by Durham County Council. Maybe it rivals Nenthead, maybe they complement each other. You can picnic at either spot if the weather is kind. If it is you could even have two picnics — one at each.

Killhope Wheel — another tourist centre. Once water powered this whole industry

In more serious style people have taken lately to exploring many of the old workings. You're not supposed to, at least without permission, because some are potentially highly dangerous. But there is a body called NORPEX, composed of mining experts of one sort or another who go in for a mixture of pot-holing and industrial archaeology.

One working in particular has interested people like these, and that is the engineering masterpiece known as the Nent Force Level.

This four-and-a-half-mile underground canal between Nenthead and Alston was built by John Smeaton (of Eddystone Lighthouse fame) between 1775 and 1839 at a cost of £80,000. One of its purposes was to drain the existing mines; the other to discover new veins. It fulfilled the first all right, but found in all those miles

and years only one really workable lead deposit. It had one other function, though—it was a great leisure attraction for the young things of the district, who could travel along it in thirty-foot gondolas by the light of candles or flaming torches. It was nine foot square and trippers could haul themselves along it by means of wooden staples set into the walls until they reached the dramatic underground waterfall below Nentsberry, which was duly admired before their return.

Thomas Sopwith of the rival Allendale empire described such a trip by the light of candles:

> "the reflection of them in the water presents a fine spectacle, and by this means also, some idea is afforded of the vast extent of the level by the receding vista of lights. In the daytime

the level mouth is seen from upwards of a mile up the level; in sunshine seeming like a brilliant star with radiating beams. At such time also, the faint and straggling day-beams give to the rugged outline and green mosses of the roof and sides the same subdued but silvery brightness, which, in immediate contrast with the surrounding darkness, has the same poetical character, the same inimitable effect, as that with which the beautiful ruins of Melrose are now forever associated."

He was a fine mining engineer was Tommy Sopwith, but as a writer just a little over the top perhaps.

Alston Market Cross. Handy seating for the public

The Nent Force Level is closed today, except for official exploratory groups, but there is some hope that it may one day be re-opened, when it will no doubt be described as another heritage attraction, unless we have worn that much-maltreated word completely out by then.

In early years methods of detecting the invisible presence of minerals was haphazard, not to say bizarre. Some believed that the sun and the stars somehow drew up evidence of their presence through the pores of the earth, and hazel rods were used to confirm it, rather as water-diviners work.

> "Such superficial excrescenses whether vegetable or mineral do direct the miners in their knowledge of the metals under them," wrote Sir John Petties in 1670, "which sometimes is also done by the virgula divina or magic rod, being no other than a hazel stick cut in a certain season of the stars' aspects. Still showing what rare contiguity there is between the stars, plants, animals and minerals...."

I have met old miners who claimed that surface wild flowers would indicate the presence of this metal or that below them, but by the time the Quaker Company arrived prospecting was much more scientific. Sometimes vertical shafts were drilled, as in coal-mining, but more generally tunnels were bored horizontally into the fell-side, and the veins worked upwards by means of shafts called sumps. Miners climbed up these chimneys by wooden stemples set in their sides, and dropped down the ore they extracted into wagons below. It is the depth of some of these sumps which presents the main danger to the unwary or inexperienced today.

So Alston in the nineteenth century had become quite a prosperous little town, with an endowed grammar school, among the quainter activities of whose scholars was cock-fighting for a prayer-book each Easter. What would today's churches have to say if that gentle old custom was revived?

The turn into the twentieth century was by no means kind to Alston. The bottom dropped out of lead, gradually, bumpily. There was a woollen mill, employing at its height eighty workers, and this became an iron foundry which in turn closed down in 1980. Today it is used on a rather smaller scale to make precision castings in metal. And that's about it, except for tourism, that

double-edged hope for so many places today.

Even in these days of heritage centres, crafte shoppes and kindred visitor-bait, Alston gives the impression of being a little ambivalent about the blessings of the tourist trade. If it was not for its presence at a strategic junction on the A686 road linking Tyneside with the Lake District, it might catch rather little, but now both the Pennine Way and the C2C bike track draw hundreds of the more active brand of travellers every year.

There is a youth hostel at Alston as well as residential pubs and bed-and-breakfast establishments, but they don't overdo the slicker come-into-my-parlour techniques of most traditional holiday towns.

St. Augustine's and Alston Centre

Chapter Three

Alston to Knarsdale

All aboard the South Tyne Special — three miles there and three back

One aspect of Alston's past which, ironically, has proved of more interest since it was killed off than during its lifetime, is the railway line between the town and the main Carlisle-Newcastle line down the South Tyne Valley to Haltwhistle. Route might be a better word than line, for few things disappear more quickly than railway track once condemned, nothing is so transitory as 'permanent way'. Alston's branch line was opened in 1852 when railway optimism was at its peak. It was in its early years used mainly to transport the lead which for centuries had been carried over the fells by pack-pony teams, and such was the enthusiasm of the time that there was even talk of linking Alston with Weardale to the south over steep Killhope. This was not long after Sir John MacAdam had planted a turnpike road over this wild tract to replace what he himself said was the worst road he had ever seen. He also built the road over Hartside Pass to the west., now beloved by squadrons of fast motor-bikers whose affection is rarely requited by locals and other road-users.

As it turned out, railway optimism didn't last long. As lead production fell, so did the railway company's profits, indeed it made none at all during the twentieth century, and in 1976 it was closed down. It says little for the prescience of Dr. Beeching and his henchmen that the same line now draws over 16,000 visitors every year.

Alston Station has been preserved, and a band of enthusiastic amateurs has been busy for some years now laying down a narrow-gauge track along the old route, carrying punters on little steam-trains all of three miles up to the county boundary at Gilderdale and back.

They work in their spare time, these railway buffs, both staffing the locomotives and pushing the track back out gradually, yard by yard, at weekends or during their holidays. There is talk of extending the line still further down the valley, and even of re-opening it all the way to Haltwhistle, some fifteen miles away. Meantime first Northumberland County Council, then

SUSTRANS have opened it up as the South Tyne Trail, for walkers and riders.

The route follows closely the flow of the South Tyne north of Alston, through a landscape of wild, rolling fells fringed at the bottom with a vegetation almost lush for this part of the world. This is an ancient route. No doubt the old Britons used it, although we are told that they often preferred to keep to the higher ground, and the Romans marched along it, building one of their main trunk routes from the South up to Carvoran on what was to become Hadrian's Wall.

A metalled turnpike road followed in more recent times west of the river, and another narrower road parallels it on the east through the hamlet with the delightful name of Ale. More recently still the Pennine Way long-distance footpath uses it, incorporating for some miles a stretch of the Roman Maiden Way. Walking it now on a wet and windy day you can imagine the exploratory feelings of those first troops of Julius Agricola, wondering what the gods had in store for them over the next bleak rise.

Sporting country now, all this section. There are grouse moors on either side and both salmon and sea-trout are caught in the river below. The fish appear rather later in the season than in most English waters, but this is to be expected when you work out that they have to swim nearly eighty miles from the North Sea for the privilege of being hooked up in the North Pennines. Anglers are usually given to grumbling, but it seems to be a fact these days that more fish are being caught in these stretches than for most of the past two centuries, since heavy industry down

Whitley Castle housed Roman troops from all over the known world

near the Tyne's mouth was cleaned up or, more often, closed down. Little enough shipbuilding at Wallsend and Jarrow any more, but South Tyne salmon are flourishing. Engineering workers have lost their jobs, but the anglers can now get more sport. It's a funny old world.

With the Whitfield fells stretching over to the next major valley, Allendale, to the east, and the slopes of Grey Nag and the Three Pikes rolling up to Cold Fell to the west, just three miles out of Alston on the latter side stands what is left of Whitley Castle, a Roman outpost fort which seems to have no Latin name as most had.

One suggestion has been that it was the *Alione* of the Third Cohort of the *Nervii* (the tribe that Caesar overcame in Mark Antony's speech), but whatever its name, it must have been a most

welcome stopping-place for marching troops on their way to the Wall after a hard slog over the cold shoulder of Cross Fell.

Whitley Castle is also unlike most Roman forts in that it is not quadrilateral but trapezoid, or lozenge-shaped. It stands under the ridge and is hemmed by banks of earthworks. Little serious excavation has taken place at Whitley Castle, but an altar dedicated to Hercules was found in the fort's burial ground at the beginning of the nineteenth century. Also bits of shoe-leather, a copper breast-pin, various domestic tools and a length of pipe. It's made of lead, but this does not conclusively prove that it was necessarily lead mined or smelted hereabouts.

Below the fort, and on the other side of the A689, is the tiny hamlet of Kirkhaugh whose kirk or

19

church, on the haugh or water-meadow, is on the far side of the river and was reached from the village only by stepping-stones. There is now a proper little bridge marking the concept of rural progress, though the congregation is doubtless smaller now than in the stepping-stones day.

There is no parish church at Slaggyford, the next village proper in the dale, but there is one a mile or so further north at Knarsdale. Neither is there a pub at Slaggy these days, but the Kirkstyle at Knarsdale provides refreshment for fishermen, Pennine Way walkers and the intrepid shooters of grouse.

The kirk in this case is that of St. Jude, patron saint of lost causes. It was built in 1838 on the foundations of a previous church, and its antiquity is indicated by tombstones in the yard of two Jacobite sympathisers, and possibly by the grave of one Robert Baxter, who died in October, 1796 and was buried here. Or was he?

His epitaph, according to William Weaver Tomlinson in his little masterpiece, the *Comprehensive Guide to Northumberland*, first published towards the end of the nineteenth century, tells how Baxter was murdered up on the fell by being given a poisoned sandwich, and ends with the line:

"I hope he will rewarded be / That laid the poison there for me."

Very unusual, that a tombstone which carried a curse should have been allowed in a consecrated burial place. But was it? I have had a good look round Knarsdale Churchyard, but I can't find it. Nor do the local church-people seem to know where it is, although they vaguely remember having heard of it. Yet something of the sort must have existed, or Tomlinson wouldn't have been able to quote it: even writers of guidebooks don't as a rule make such things up, however much they may borrow or steal from each other. And could this be the answer? Tomlinson mentions an earlier writer, the Chartist leader Eneas Mackenzie of Newcastle, who published in 1827 and quotes his book. Could it be that for religious or family reasons, the mysterious tombstone was removed some time after it was first written

St. Jude's Church

about, and that Tomlinson hadn't bothered to check? Stranger things have happened in country churchyards.

There is less mystery about another St. Jude's headstone — that dedicated to 'The Vagabond'. This was the pen-name of one Alex Wills, a Newcastle man who during the thirties roamed and camped all over the countryside and wrote a number of very popular booklets about his travels in the district. He eventually settled in Slaggyford, where he died. Of the sociability of the local people he wrote:

"These deep, long glens did not lend themselves to the military requirements of early ages; militarily it was a guerrilla warfare country. But it missed even that and went peacefully on with what agriculture the fertile clearings afforded. Saved from warlike bloodshed and violence its story flows gently, and its peoples reflect it."

Some historians might disagree with this assessment of the valley's gentleness, but the Vagabond had to live with it.

But I have leapfrogged a bit, not having finished with Slaggyford, which is a straggling little village at the foot of the ridge on Thornhope Fell on the west side of the river. One or two of its

Ancient bell pits above Knarsdale

houses are of a fair age, and indeed the place was once quite important, having an annual fair and a weekly market. Not that you would dream of any such things today. Slaggy is one of our might-a-beens. Apparently some time in the nineteenth century a grocer from Alston had a dream which told him, night after night, that Slaggyford was sitting on a fortune of lead. The grocer spent a lot of money sinking a shaft, but found nothing. The village sank back into obscurity until the railway arrived in the 1850s, when it acquired its own station, only to sink back once more when the line closed. What happened to the Alston grocer is not recorded. Perhaps one of his backers poisoned him with a sandwich too.

Perhaps, though, if he had been a little better versed in geology and not so obsessed, like a lot of his neighbours, with the great god Galena, he would have realised that Slaggyford was sitting, if not on a bonanza, at least on quite reasonable deposits of coal. And it had been mined around here for some considerable time. In a low evening light you can still see today, on the opposite side of the valley, lines of circular depressions which were once the bell pits that the early miners used before they had the technology to venture far underground. They just dug a hole into a coal outcrop and went down and in until it ran out. They widened the hole only just as much as safety would allow, leaving a hole shaped like the inside of a bell. When the sides round the top looked like falling in, they moved on and dug another hole.

But coal and lead were not the only minerals wrought along these hilltops. Cropping out along the 500-metre contour on the fells above Knarsdale is a band of grey millstone rock where, many years ago, men would cut their circular prizes *in situ* and roll the completed stones down to the valley for use in grinding corn. Sometimes they shattered before this and a number of unsuccessful efforts lie around to this day.

Smashed millstone above Knarsdale

Chapter Four

Knarsdale to the A69

Tows Bank. Disused colliery in the woods

Coal is still mined around here. There are a couple of small, privately-run pits just outside Alston itself, and one or two others along the river valley. Old-time rural style collieries these, set in the woods, and they tend to come and go. The seams grow more productive the further north the river runs. There were bigger collieries at Lambley, Midgeholme and down at

Packhorse bridge at Lambley colliery. Stephenson's Rocket made its last journey under it

Haltwhistle itself, the next town of any size. At Coanwood on the east side of the river there were collieries and coke ovens, whose fires showed up for miles in the night skies. They closed way before the war, most of the population moved to pits further down the Tyne, and Coanwood today shows no sign of having ever been anything more than a quiet cluster of houses, a school and a couple of farms .

There were other coal mines all along the Pennine foothills going west over towards Brampton, where the earls of Carlisle had their pits under Cold Fell. Not strictly South Tyne

Valley this, but it linked to it with a spur off the Alston-Haltwhistle railway along which George Stephenson's famous 'Rocket' made its final working journey when it was roped in to act as a stationary haulage engine working the inclined-planes of Lord Carlisle's fellside pits. These old collieries have been finished for a long time, but there is a touching memorial to their existence by the roadside near Hallbankgate.

"James William Walton, hewer, who was killed by flooding at the Roach Burn Mine........ And of Robert Pattinson, deputy overman, and Matthew Hilliard, back overman, who bravely

The Roach Burn memorial near Hallbankgate

returned to the pit and gave up their own lives in the attempt to rescue their comrade. January 28, 1908."

Above the names, on a plaque in the cross of red sandstone, it adds:

"Greater love hath no man than this...."

The Roach Burn memorial hasn't the appalling numbers listed on disaster columns in the coalfields of Durham and industrial Tyneside, but the story is no less poignant for its small size.

Modern mining technology is too impatient to be bothered much with the sinking of shafts, the ventilation of new workings and the foundation of small communities. On the other side of the South Tyne, at Plenmeller, which is pushing over towards the Allendale fells, the National Coal Board started in the late nineteen-eighties to opencast for coal under the peat and heather.

Rip the top off, gouge down deep, and howk it all out, like opening up a pie-crust to get at the steak and kidney. They worked daily round the clock, under arc-lights when it got dark, and they finished the whole job before the turn of the Millennium, by which time the Coal Board had gone and the private firm of J.M. Budge had taken over. Before they began to reinstate the surface, it was a weird feeling to stand at the bottom of the great hole they had dug, actually among the seams previous generations of miners had had to dig deep tunnels to reach. You could stand where they knelt or lay on their sides and hewed by hand in the old days in separate small pits long forgotten. They were deep underground, you were in the open air and you did not bump your back on the sky.

So far the history of the South Tyne valley has been largely industrial. But here at the north end of the Pennines, where the river takes almost a right-angled bend and starts flowing eastward along the Tyne-Solway Gap, we are getting into Border country.

Fertile land, this, by contrast with the fells, and rich pickings for the feuding tribes of cattle-thieves as well as the armies of both England and Scotland, who fought over this area for years, harrowing with spears and swords and sowing and reaping mayhem and death.

There were medieval castles built at Featherstone, Blenkinsopp, Thirlwall and Bellister, all around the town of Haltwhistle. Blenkinsopp has a coal mine under it now (closed, unfortunately in 2002), and a pub-cum-caravan-site; Bellister became a hotel, and

Bellister Castle — has its own ghost, the Grey Man

Featherstone Park, during the 1939-45 war, housed a large prison-camp for *Wehrmacht* officers.

But these castles were really needed in their early years. The village of Lambley nearby had its own Benedictine nunnery from Norman times. But in 1297 it was destroyed by the Scots during William Wallace's biggest marauding venture into England when they laid waste large parts of Northumberland.

> "In this raid they surpassed in cruelty all the fury of the heathen,"

wrote the monk-chronicler of Lanercost.

> "When they could not catch the young and strong they imbrued their arms with the blood of infirm people, old women, women in childbed, and even children two or three years old, proving themselves apt scholars in atrocity inasmuch as they raised little span-long children pierced on pikes to expire thus and fly away to the heavens."

The nuns of Lambley did not escape. "*Indignities worse than death were inflicted upon the holy sisters*," as Tomlinson puts it. But the convent was restored—for a time at least—though there were only six nuns in residence when Henry VIII suppressed the place. What Henry left was not long after washed away by the waters of the South Tyne, and today not a trace remains, except, no doubt, for stones requisitioned for later houses, particularly Lambley Farm, which sits almost on the old convent site, and also for its bell, which still hangs above the nineteenth-century church in Lambley village. There is nothing much else in it today, except a telephone kiosk, a notice-board, and the mighty nine-arched viaduct which threw the railway over the river at its narrowest point, where it cut through a steep outcrop of the Whin Sill, that huge intrusion of volcanic dolerite which stretches from Teesdale right across Northumberland, where it carries Hadrian's Wall along its crags for miles, to reappear out to sea as the Farne Islands.

There was an early British settlement on top of the crags at the eastern end of the Lambley Viaduct, which may or may not also have been a Roman signal station. The viaduct itself is 100 feet high and was getting ruinous before a thorough repair and facelift in 1996 restored its old strength but not its trains. Today it is becoming something of a visitor attraction. The South Tyne Trail runs close by and SUSTRANS hope to link it to their National Cycle Network

This stretch of the Pennine Way from Alston down the river, then over Blenkinsopp Common via parts of the Maiden Way, both the celebrated Mr. Wainwright and Tony Hopkins, who wrote the Countryside Commission's official guide, reckon is the dullest stretch of the whole walk. "*Some days are roses, others are thorns*," as the latter puts it, presumably seeing this as one of the prickly bits. True there is not a lot of variety until the Roman Wall is reached at Greenhead, but then the Way itself does not touch the town of Haltwhistle, on the busy A69 between Carlisle and Newcastle.

Lambley Viaduct. Plenty of arches, but no trains any more

Chapter Five

Haltwhistle to the confluence

Haltwhistle — centre of Britain?

Actually Haltwhistle is not strictly on the main road any more, having been by-passed in 1997, so that what was once a dangerously narrow half-mile of Victorian housing is now strangely quiet, and the shopkeepers up in the centre complain of falling trade.

Haltwhistle, for all its nineteenth-century workaday looks, is really quite an ancient place. Its name, which sounds as if it might have been conjured up by some Victorian railwayman, was once spelled *Hautwyesill* and is said to mean (though in precisely what language is not explained) 'the holy hill of the high water', or 'the high watch-hill or beacon'. This according to Tomlinson. You takes your choice. The locals call it 'Halty'.

There certainly was a hill — still is of course — at the east end called the Castle Hill, which seems once to have been fortified. And there was the Musgrove Tower, 'the Old Tower of Hautwysill' behind it. It stood opposite the present Spotted Cow pub, but it was demolished in 1963. There may have been more: certainly it would have been unusual for a settlement holding such a strategic position in the Middle Ages not to have been well defended, and there were a number of pele towers or bastle-houses along the main street, the most impressive being the present Centre of Britain, once the Red Lion Hotel.

Certain proof of the town's antiquity comes from the Church of the Holy Cross, dating back to the twelfth century. Its chancel was built about that time, and the nave is of the thirteenth. There is a crusader's tomb, remembering Thomas, a member of the Blenkinsopp family during the long Border troubles. Even now the church hardly shows itself above the shops and offices in the little market place, but peeps through shyly in the gaps between them.

King Edward I rested here in 1306 on his last journey to try finally to hammer the Scots. As a sort of legacy he left the little town the right to hold hiring fairs twice a year, in May and November, which like Newcastle's annual festivity, became known as 'The Hoppings'. But Edward was an old, sick man, and he was to die early the following year at Burgh-by-Sands within sight across the Solway of the land he tried so hard to subdue. In the turbulent times which followed, and of which he was at least partly the cause, Haltwhistle can never have been far from, or long out of, the action. There is a

Haltwhistle Church — crusader's tomb inside

famous old ballad called *The Fray of Hautwessel* which begins:

> The limmer thieves o' Liddesdale
> Wadna leave a kye in the hail countrie,
> But an' we gie them the caud steel
> Our gear they'll reive it a' awaye;
> Sae pert they stealis I you say:
> O' late they came to Hautwessel,
> And thowt they there wad drive a fray,
> But Alec Ridley shot too well....

And there's a lot more in the same vein and with similar spelling, but in the end Alec Ridley shoots

Haltwhistle, going upmarket under the arches

Wat Armstrong in the eye: "*Went through his steel cap, heid and a'*" and the Liddesdale reivers retired with a warning not to come back again, which doubtless they took little notice of.

Haltwhistle is comparatively peaceful today. Before the war it was a mining community, but its pits have long since been closed. It was saved from mass unemployment by the establishment of some light industry—plastic bottles, antifreeze and paint mostly. But it still hasn't quite lost the feel of a colliery town. Three social clubs there are, as well as half a dozen pubs, leek shows and all. But just lately it has been tip-toeing a little up market. It now advertises itself as the heart of the Roman Wall Country, and indeed old Hadrian's bulwark is only a couple of miles up the hill; it has its own glossy pamphlet advertising its own 'Reivers' Trail', and it has recently twinned itself with the Breton town of St. Meen-le-Grand. The Pennine Way avoids Haltwhistle, but it is handy for walkers' refreshment and accommodation.

So many books have been written about the Roman occupation of this part of Britain, both scholarly and popular, that I shall commend readers to them and stick to the lower ground of the Tyne Valley itself. Which takes us next to Bardon Mill, a small village which had until some time in the 1980s the westernmost NCB colliery in Northumberland. There were smaller pits even further west, as we have seen, but they were privately run, being considered too small to warrant continued management by the nationalised concern. That some of these mines are still producing while Bardon Mill and the others are dead no doubt proves something, and old miners round here will tell you there is still much coal left below ground,. Without its pit Bardon Mill carries on as a little by-passed village with a pub and a railway station, and a pottery converted from a former woollen mill.

Above Bardon Mill, up the hill, are the remains of the Roman station of Vindolanda on the Stanegate, Agricola's road from Carvoran in the west to Chesters near the confluence of the South and North Tynes, and pre-dating Hadrians Wall by some forty years. It's an interesting place, Vindolanda, with a museum and visible remains of its fort. It is also under continual excavation,

and Robin Birley and his team have unearthed some unique clues to the military and domestic life of the early occupants, including a lengthy and fascinating correspondence by one of the commandants' wives written on birch-bark notepaper.

Back down through Bardon Mill and over on the other side of the river is what is left of the castle of Willimontswick, which has been incorporated into a modern house. It was once the home of the Ridley family (they of the Fray of Haltwhistle, no doubt), important folk in these parts, and including Nicholas Ridley, Bishop of

Beltingham Church — another for St. Cuthbert

London, who was martyred at Oxford in 1555, being burnt at the stake with his friend Hugh Latimer by order of Mary Tudor.

A mile eastward is the little church of St. Cuthbert at Beltingham, the only Northumbrian church to be built entirely in the Perpendicular style (although additions were made later and rather overdone). It was supposed to have been once the personal chapel of the Ridleys, which would show how important they were, and that name crops up in even greater splendour at Ridley Hall, now a students' residence, but set in magnificent grounds on the banks of the River Allen near its confluence with the South Tyne, and a favourite walk for visitors.

"Nowhere in the county," writes our Mr. Tomlinson in a fine splash of Victorian purple,

> "has Nature arranged more harmoniously her wonderful effects of wood and rock and water than in these beautiful and extensive grounds."

And so, with the A69, the Carlisle-Newcastle railway, and the river running intertwined like three strands in a length of electric flex, the little town, or large village, of Haydon Bridge is reached in its lush valley with the Roman Wall out of sight now but just five miles or so above. You might look at Haydon Bridge today and believe it to be one big settlement for the young, for secondary school pupils from miles around

Haydon Bridge — fish, chips and eccentrics

are bussed and trained in daily to the County High School, and the fish and chip shop does a good scholastic trade.

But then education was always important round here. There was a Free School started in 1685 by a local vicar who had come into a little money, and by what sounds like shrewd investment built up its funds over the years until it could afford four teachers, a headmaster who had to be an MA (and presumably a clergyman, for he had to lead morning service every other Sunday). They were well paid too, for those days: £250 a year for the Head, and houses with gardens for the teaching staff.

Haydon Bridge has also been a great place for eccentrics. There was Ned Coulson the celebrated nineteenth-century runner, who used to play the fiddle as he ran, but behind his back to make it more difficult if not melodious. And in quite a different class was John Martin, otherwise known as Mad Martin.

Mad Martin was born at East Landends Farm, which still stands right by the south bank of the river just outside Haydon Bridge, part of a quite remarkable family. His mother claimed to be descended from the Ridleys, and seems to have been a woman of strong character. Her eldest son William was an inventor, with mining lamps a speciality. He also wrote poetic jingles and called himself an 'Anti-Newtonian Philosopher and Conqueror of All Nations'.

The second, Jonathan, was a great fire-raiser, with the burning of York Minster his most spectacular arson achievement; and the next,

John, was a painter of apocalyptic scenes, who in the early nineteenth-century became for a while the most popular artist in Britain.

He went to school at Haydon Bridge, where he sketched in the sand beneath the bridge itself, and mixed a mud pigment to paint portraits of the family cat. Later he was apprenticed to a coach-builder in Newcastle before going off to London where he became famous. He painted great violent biblical scenes like the Flood and the Last Judgement, with Newcastle's Norman Keep dominating the skyline of old Jerusalem. And he painted celestial themes like *The Plains of Heaven*. He claimed to have got his horror visions from the mines round about his early home, his idea of Paradise from the scenery of Tynedale.

He wished, he once said, that he had become an engineer instead, and indeed he spent much of his time designing improvements to London's sewage and transport systems, as well as having decided opinions about mines ventilation and safety which sometimes clashed with those of the powerful George Stephenson (who was born just a few miles further down the Tyne at Wylam), but which were subsequently vindicated.

He was, in short, an all-round man, self-made too, some would have said, except that he made no money out of his social improvement ideas, and didn't seem to care whether he made any or not. Which is probably why they called him Mad Martin.

In Martin's time Haydon Bridge was very much

on the lead trade's route. Pack horse teams wound down from the heights of Alston Moor and the Allendales to a big smelt mill at Langley, from where the refined ingots were taken down the Tyne to Newcastle. Langley was once part of the fiefdom of the Radcliffe family, and there is a wayside cross on the lane down to Haydon Bridge.

'To the memory of James and Charles, Viscounts Langley, Earls of Derwentwater, beheaded on Tower Hill, London.... for loyalty to their lawful sovereign.'

Nearby is Langley Castle, which the Radcliffes also owned before their downfall. It was built in 1350 by one Sir Thomas de Lucy as a stronghold against the Scots It was ruined—ironically by the English army of Henry IV, according to Tomlinson—and by remaining a ruin until bought by the local antiquary Cadwallader Bates in the nineteenth century, escaped piecemeal additions and retained

"in an almost, if not quite unique, manner the essential outlines of a fortified English house in the great days of Cressy and Poitiers,"

according to Mr. Bates. Langley Castle is remarkable for having three tiers of latrines in one wall,

one above the other and staggered, discharging into the ditch outside. Either the owners ate and drank excessively well, or the place was used to housing garrisons rather larger than normal.

Langley Castle — medieval knights out

35

In more recent years Langley Castle became a girls' private school and, later still, a venue for mock-medieval banquets, where coachloads of the good people of Tyneside could carouse on a Saturday night in what they imagined to be the style of the medieval barons, to say nothing of their ladies. Today it is an hotel and restaurant, described in latest Newspeak as *'The Langley Castle Experience.'*

Few people from outside this area will have heard of the little village of Newbrough. Yet once, for just a couple of months, it was, technically I suppose, the capital of England. For Edward I, on his last journey which finished up by the Solway in 1307, stayed resting here by the Tyne with all his army and court around him. You would never guess at royal connections today, though.

Fourstones, an old quarrying village nearby, has a paper mill. Limestone was dug at Frankham Fell, and sandstone at Prudham, much of this product finishing up in important buildings in London and Glasgow. Fourstones is supposed to have got its name from the presence years ago of four Roman altars which marked its boundaries before disappearing.

No doubt during their stay by the haughs of the Tyne some of King Edward's more energetic soldiers or courtiers would have passed the time walking up Warden Hill, which rises above the dale. It's only just over 500 feet high, but it commands most of the countryside around. On its top are the earthworks of a two-acre British hill-fort. From here Edward's men, and their ancestors before them, and us for that matter, could look all the way back up the South Tyne to the Northern Pennines which gave it birth.

They—we—could see more, for at the foot of Warden Hill the North Tyne comes bubbling in to join its twin.

But the North Tyne is another story.

Part Two — The North Tyne

Chapter One
The Twin Tynes

North meets South

I have often wondered why as kids we got so excited about the Wild West, why we spent hour after dark hour sitting in stuffy cinemas watching tobacco-chewing gentlemen with funny hats and even funnier accents gunning each other down with hardly a drop of blood to show for it, when we had the same story here on our own doorstep, minus the baccy.

Why make up stories about Billy the Kid and Bonnie and Clyde when we had Archie

Armstrong and Kinmont Willie in our own backyard? The real thing. We had our own Wild West — well, until recently. Our own Wild North if you want to be literal — the Border between England and Scotland where for hundreds of years there was nothing but trouble of, I don't doubt, a highly colourful nature. Where life was cheap, nasty, brutish and short.

The whole region lived on the rustling of sheep and cattle and whole families, tribes really, were at blood feud with each other for generations. Today the region is at peace — all good neighbours together. But in the old days it was different. It was Tynedale against Liddesdale against Redesdale; Armstrongs mortal foes of Grahams, Charltons, Milburns, Fenwicks, Robsons (*'honest men, save doing a little shifting for their living, God and Our Lady help them, silly poor men'*) all forming temporary alliances against the others and just as swiftly breaking them.

North Tyne — peaceful today but flowing from troubled old waters

Bridge at Chollerford, but the Romans got there first

Territorial limits were just as unsettled as the people. Tynedale was sometimes in England, other times in Scotland. This was almost a country in its own right — the Borderland.

The River North Tyne was as wild as anywhere in the Borders: a natural enough state of affairs, as it was the most clearly-defined way right through that country, a natural route for men on the warpath, whether full armies or small gangs of desperadoes after food and wealth and women.

The river rises on what is the Scottish Border today, and flows down for forty miles to join the South Tyne in the lush lands near Hexham. It was hereabouts that its story started, when the Romans built a bridge across it at Chollerford — the first proper bridge it ever had. They built it within sight of Warden Hill, where the ancient Brits had a fine camp dominating the country for miles around.

It overlooked all three Tynes — the South, away to its origins among the high Pennines of Cumbria, the North, up to the land of the Picts and the Scots, and to the east the fruit of their union, the Tyne itself, ploughing on strongly down to the sea beyond what would, long after, become Newcastle.

The Newcastle-Carlisle railway line — with Warden Hill in the background

Chapter Two
Chollerford

Chesters bath-house — clean-up for muddy Romans

There were early settlements right up the North Tyne on both sides, but the river's recorded history started, as did so much of it in these wild parts, with the Romans. They used their bridge to carry the line of Hadrian's Wall over the water. As well as a bridge they built a fort which they called Cilurnum, which became known years after their departure as simply 'Chesters', or 'Camps'. In its heyday it housed a cavalry regiment 500 strong from Asturias in northern Spain, from between the Picos de Europa and the Bay of Biscay. The late Professor Eric Birley described Chesters as the best example of a cavalry fort visible anywhere in the Roman

Empire, and although only part of it has yet been exposed, it is clear from its sheer size that it was of great importance. As was usual with forts along the line of the wall, a large part of the station protruded outside it, with gates allowing for rapid exits to raid barbarian lands to the north.

Visible today are parts of the barracks and stables, the headquarters building in the centre, and the commandant's quarters and bath-house,

with another bath-house for lower ranks outside the walls between the camp and the river. The remains of the gateways can also be seen, but what make Chesters unique are the remains of the Roman bridge.

The North Tyne has changed its course over the centuries, so that the west abutment is now under water, and the east is high and dry on the far bank, though it can be more closely inspected

The remains of the Roman Bridge at Chesters

by walking from the east end of the modern road bridge at Chollerford. One of the cutwaters has an easily-recognised phallic symbol carved in it, pointing upstream, as if a crude symbol of derision to the northern tribes, equivalent to today's two-fingered salute—who knows?

The site of Chesters Fort, and the nineteenth-century mansion by its entrance, were owned by the Clayton family, and house a fine little museum with a unique collection of Roman altars and carvings, not only from Cilurnum itself, but from other parts of the Wall. For John

Clayton, who succeeded his father Nathaniel as the progressive Town Clerk of Newcastle in its planning heyday (their name lives still in one of the city's more important streets), was an enthusiastic archaeologist, who probably did more to preserve the Wall last century than any man or department. Today the Chesters site is in the capable hands of English Heritage, and open to the public as one of their main showplaces.

There are, as might be expected, other Roman remains in the area. The Stanegate, the east-west road which pre-dated the Wall itself, passed nearby and crossed the river here, and in the hamlet of Brunton on the east side of the river is a seven-foot-high section of the Wall with the finest example in all its length of one of its regular turrets.

The Turret at Brunton

A considerable civilian settlement built up, as was usual, outside the walls of Cilurnum fort. It would have housed small tradesmen and merchants who would usually have been certain during the 300 years or so of military occupation, of a steady custom from the relatively well, and sometimes regularly, paid troops. There were no doubt pubs of one sort or another, and establishments known by a rather earthier name than the 'massage-parlours' of modern times. No traces remain today above ground, although the general outline of the village has been photographed from the air during unusually dry summers. One good thing the Clayton family did was to put a stop to the robbing of Roman structures for ready-dressed stone. Before their time the ruins had been used as a cheap and handy quarry, and many of the older houses in this area, and the churches, were constructed largely of masonry from the wall. Appropriately, the little village on the road down to Hexham is called just that—Wall. The church of St. Michael and All Angels in the village of Warden, by the confluence ('a sweet and retired little village', according to Tomlinson), is full of Roman stone, and particularly in its eleventh-century tower and thirteenth century transepts. Like many in this lawless country, it served as much as a defensive tower as a house of worship.

Near to Chollerford, off the B6318 Military Road to Newcastle, is reputed to be the site where the saintly King Oswald of Northumbria raised a cross before his victory over the pagan Welsh king Cadwallon of Gwynneth at the Battle of Heavenfield. The Venerable Bede ascribes the Christian victory to the presence of this cross:

> "for we know that there was no emblem of the Christian Faith, no church, no altar, in the whole of Bernicia...."

According to Bede this cross was hurriedly made and the king himself held it in position in its hole while his soldiers rammed in earth around it.

> "This done, he summoned his army with a loud shout, crying: 'Let us kneel together, and ask the true and living God Almighty of His mercy to protect us from the arrogant savagery of our enemies, since He knows that we fight in a just cause to save our nation.'"

Oswald was not the first, and certainly not the last, general to recruit the Creator to his side, and he must have been on the right lines for, as Bede tells us, many miracles followed.

> "Many folk take splinters of wood from this holy cross, which they put into water, and when any sick men or beasts drink of it or are sprinkled with it, they are at once restored to health."

There's a modern cross today at the side of the Military Road above Chollerford and a signboard telling you a bit about Heavenfield. Behind them in a field is a little eighteenth century chapel, restored in the nineteenth, dedicated of course to St. Oswald.

Oswald's successor as King of Northumbria was Oswin, another saint. This was the period when this region was the crucible of a resurgent western Christianity, but this state of things was not to last.

Affairs seem to have gone from bad to worse in the Dark Ages, but the wall of Hadrian, however knocked about, remained as a boundary. Below it was a semblance of law and order and the rule of law; upstream, the land of the barbarians once more, of those literally beyond the pale. North Tynedale was to stay outside English law for centuries. The King's Writ did not run north of the Wall until the reign of George III just 200 years ago. And traditionally the merchants of Newcastle are said to have refused to apprentice any lad born in Tynedale or Redesdale, which was an even wilder branch of it.

Chapter Three

Houghton, Chipchase and Simonburn

Haughton Castle gateway — easier in than out

Some semblance of authority had to be stamped on such a lawless area, and it fell into the hands of local chieftains and war-lords, the heads of the more successful families, which would have meant the hardest, most ruthless of a ruthless lot. They built their fortresses as big and as strong as they could afford. Some were mere pele towers or bastle-houses, little more than fortified farmsteads—ground floor for livestock, upper rooms for defence of the family.

Others were quite elaborate strongholds, like Haughton Castle, which guarded the confluence of the twin Tynes near Humshaugh. They were strung along, these defensive buildings, right up the North Tyne Valley like rough beads on a grim old necklace. They've all got their legends, and some no doubt their ghosts. Haughton has both.

Its story goes that during the reign of Henry VIII, when Tynedale was still no better than it should have been, it was held by Sir Thomas Swinburne, an ancestor of the poet. He had captured a notorious Scottish bandit (or patriot, depending on which country you came from) called Archie Armstrong, and, following the sort of hospitality current in these parts, threw him into a deep dungeon. En suite it would have been, in a way: that is, it would have had its own running water—down the walls. Its cuisine, though, was hardly top-class, as the wretched Archie Armstrong was soon to find out.

Swinburne had to go to York to see Cardinal Wolsey about some Border trouble or other, and

Haughton Castle — where Archie Armstrong met a hungry end

rode off quite forgetting his guest. It was not until he was waiting to be admitted to the great prelate that he remembered, and, as some people today might think of the family dog, recalled that he had not left any instructions about having him fed.

Now most Border lords in those days would have given the matter no further thought, but Sir Thomas must have been a kindly sort of man for the age he lived in, for he started back to Haughton without even seeing the cardinal, which sounds a risky enough thing to have done, humanity or not. Alas, his return was too late. His prisoner had starved to death, in spite of having gnawed the flesh from his own arms in his hunger. Afterwards his tormented, and not to say ravenous, spirit haunted Haughton Castle with loud groans and shrieks until exorcised with the aid of a black-lettered Gothic Bible.

Which story may or may not have had some truth. But surely people like the moss-trooping Armstrongs didn't give up as easily as that. Men on hunger-strike in these softer times have lived for a month without solid food, certainly without nibbling their own limbs. But perhaps the water had dried up, and anyway it all goes to show that you should leave neither pet nor prisoner without a full bowl and daily exercise.

There was a sequel to the story. The Armstrongs rode down from their native Liddesdale to settle the score, plundering Haughton Castle and knocking it about so badly that it was described in the survey of 1541 as being in great decay.

Haughton Castle today is in private hands, and occupied, having been extensively repaired in the eighteenth century. The original stronghold dates back to the thirteenth century, when this part of the country was in the hands of the Scots. It is immensely strong, its walls eight feet thick in places, and it stands on steep high ground above a long bend on the west bank of the North Tyne. There seems to be no record of its having undergone any subsequent assaults or sieges, though it is believed to have been damaged by fire at some stage in its long past. John Dobson, architect of nineteenth-century Newcastle, and planning partner with Clayton of the Chesters, restored it. Traditionally a small ferry linked it with the village of Barrasford opposite. This is marked on the older Ordnance Survey maps, but seems since to have disappeared. Still there, however, are the remnants of a late eighteenth-century paper mill, where French currency was once forged in an attempt to devalue the revolutionary economy. For it is not by the sword alone that nation makes war upon nation.

Further upstream from Haughton, and on the opposite side of the water, is the even more impressive looking castle of Chipchase. It started off as an unusually massive pele in the bad old times, but later was added to in fine Jacobean style. For a while it was the seat (or perch perhaps) of the Heron family, of which Sir George, one-time Keeper of Tynedale and High Sheriff of Northumberland, was killed in a Border scrap which became known as the Raid of Reedswire (or the Redeswire Fray as the Ordnance Survey marks it, right on the Border by Carter Bar). This was not a haphazard fight — not to start with, anyway. It was one of a whole series of regular meetings at which men from both England and Scotland met, under the jurisdiction of the Wardens of the Marches, to settle disputes as peaceably as possible. The Redeswire meeting of 1576 started off well enough, as an old ballad tells us:

Yett was our meeting meek enough
Begun wi' merriment and mowes,
And at the braes abeun the heugh
The clerk sat down to call the rowes,
And some for kyne and some for ewes
Call'd in of Dandrie, Hob and Jock—
We saw come marching ower the knowes
Five hundred Fenwicks in a flock.

With jack and speir and bows all bent,

And warlike weapons at their will;
Yet, by my troth, we fear'd no ill.
Some gaed to drink, and some stude still,
And some to cards and dice them sped....

But it all ended in tears. As well as Heron five other of the English top-brass were killed, for only one Scot. The Tynedale men were chased back three miles into their own territory, and 600 head of their cattle were driven off the other way.

After the fight the Scots celebrated by making presents of falcons to their English prisoners, saying that their old foes could think themselves lucky since they had got live hawks for dead herons. Scottish humour has made a few advances since those days.

Chipchase Castle — pele tower to stately home

St. Mungo's, Simonburn — the sloping nave

this sort of thing was getting to be an unfortunate habit on both sides of the Tyne, and it's a good thing it was stopped.

In the nineteenth century Chipchase was the home of Hugh Taylor MP, shipping magnate and a major coal-owner in the North-east and Wales—a benevolent one for a change. Today the place is still privately inhabited, although the fine gardens are open to the public on certain days, and it is easily visible from the road.

Hopping over the river yet again (you can't really; you have to go round by Wark), there's another stately home at Nunwick Hall, seat of the Allgood family, and built in white stone in 1760. Some say it was designed by William Adam, father of the more famous brothers, but Pevsner reckons Daniel Garrett and perhaps his finest work. The Allgoods seem mostly to have been buried in the adjoining village of Simonburn, at the ancient church of St. Mungo (or Kentigern), one-time Bishop of Glasgow and a missionary in these northern English parts. The church itself was begun towards the end of the twelfth century, although there may well have been an earlier, Saxon church. An unusual feature is the distinct slope

Chipchase too had its ghost, rather similar to Haughton's haunting. This time the prisoner was one Sir Reginald FitzUrse, presumably a descendant of one of Thomas a Becket's assassins. Probably not to be outdone by their Swinburne neighbours, the Chipchase folk locked FitzUrse up and similarly forgot to look after him. So that he died, and afterwards groaned a lot, and clanked his armour. Clearly down the nave from west to east. Simonburn was in the Middle Ages the largest parish in Northumberland, running from the Roman Wall right up to Liddesdale over what is now the Scottish Border, a total of over 100 square miles. Which says not a lot for the state of religion in this part of the world.

Further evidence of Simonburn's antiquity can be found about three miles above the village, where a stone circle caps the crags of Ravensheugh. Below are the ruins of Simonburn Castle, a thirteenth-century tower with little more than part of its vaulting remaining.

Its story goes that there might have been more of it if the locals had not completely destroyed the tower looking for a treasure believed to have been big enough to have bought the whole of Northumberland. Simonburn Castle belonged at one time to the Herons of Chipchase.

St. Mungo's, Simonburn

Chapter Four

Wark and around. Ancient Britons — Brigantium

River north of Wark

There used to be a castle at Wark too, four miles further up the valley, on top of the Mote Hill which dominates the little village, and which in Celtic times was probably the meeting-place of the local elders and law-dispensers. Later, when this was part of Scotland, the Scottish kings held assize here. No signs remain today except for the steep, rounded hill itself. The only other remarkable things about Wark—on the surface at any rate—are that the main street dog-legs quite violently right in the centre, catching some motorists unawares, and that it has two of its three pubs next door to each other, the Grey Bull and the Black one. Hardly far enough apart to give much scope to police breathalysers although no doubt some folk have risked it. There is one further point of interest, come to think of it: when the lands of the Earls of Derwentwater were given, after their execution for Jacobite sympathies, to the Commissioners of Greenwich Hospital, they built Wark Church, St. Matthew's, in 1818, as a living for naval chaplains after the

Napoleonic War. They had done the same at Humshaugh further downstream.

Wark is very much the pivot of lower North Tynedale. If you want to be on the other side of the river, this is where you must cross it. Otherwise it's back south to Chollerford, or on up to Bellingham. You had to cross here too if you wanted a train. That was of course in the days when the valley had a railway, and Wark

Wark bridge — the only crossing for miles

was one of its main halts. The line ran all the way up alongside the river from Hexham to Riccarton Junction on the trans-Scottish Waverley Line, thus, in a rambling, roundabout sort of way, connecting Newcastle with Edinburgh and points north and west. Like many another railway line opened up with great optimism in the heady days of early steam locomotion, it never really made any sort of profit, and was closed in 1956, anticipating the good Dr. (later Baron) Beeching.

It has just occurred to me that it is quite possible that some of my younger readers may not be aware of the name of this man who, with government approval, destroyed a large part of our once-wonderful railway system in the 1960s and got paid for it. His name was much execrated at the time, but is now fading away to join the company of such popular baddies as the Boer chief Paul Kruger and will probably not last as long. But back to our North Tyne line:

Things must have looked pretty bright at the start, because not only were townsfolk from the industrial Tyne beginning to move out on weekend excursions in search of a bit of peace and fresh air, but both coal and iron were being mined further upstream, and a number of important stone quarries were working on the eastern bank around Gunnerton and Barrasford.

These quarries of road-metal whinstone provided most of the non-agricultural work in the area, and are still busily important today; the main difference being that the stone has now to be carried by wagon on narrow, winding roads. Such is progress.

The principal quarries are bang in the middle of an area which, in its way, could be at least as interesting historically as anything the Romans left behind them. At one time, both before and after Agricola, the slopes above this valley, particularly on its eastern side, were well populated, and there are many traces still of forts from the time of the Iron Age, and the remains of hut-circles within them.

The most evident of these can be seen on the crags above Gunnerton, at Camp hill a little to its north, and around the village of Birtley, opposite Wark. There is precious little to guide the visitor, but perhaps that is no bad thing, since it means that there are no coachloads of trippers such as flood Hadrian's Wall sites not far off. It's a bit of a puzzle to try to figure out why people visit certain ancient monuments—why one and not another. The Roman Wall, you might say, is after all just a long pile of stones. Apart from the fact that it sits in such spectacular scenery, it must give people a buzz out of its sheer antiquity (surely it can't be its weather). But it's also a link with our ancestors who actually lived through the Roman occupation.

So why not the Ancient Brits? Not just the Stonehenge builders: they were extra special, their work very evident still to all, if not its reason. But what about places like Gunnar Heugh, and the camps at Carry House and the Dene near Birtley? Places where people lived in

Gunnerton — the mounds hide an old British fort

huts before, during and after the Roman occupation, who may have fought them at first, then befriended, learnt from them, and prospered because of them. There are plenty such sites, not too evident if you don't know what you're looking for, but few people have treated them as sacred ground—not the farmers or quarry-men at any rate.

Yet the men who made these settlements and lived in them are numbered among our ancestors just as much as those who maintained the Roman military machine and the castles of the Middle Ages. Perhaps my great, great, great-recurring grandfather and grandmother lived here and had their brief being, and thought as much of their wattle-and-mud hut with a bit of the latest smart heather thatch as anyone thinks today of a new semi on a bijou estate. No mortgage either.

Perhaps I had some great-aunt a hundred times removed living a bit further up still, beyond Redesmouth, where a valley even more notorious for its lawlessness joined Tynedale. Redesdale

54

Brigantium — mock-up of fortified ancient British farmstead

travels north-eastward up beyond Otterburn nearly to the Border at Carter Bar, and it is in its upper reaches that a small museum has recently been opened at High Rochester, hard by the Roman fort of Bremenium, but dedicated to the lives and times of our early British forebears

Called Brigantium, a name conjured fancifully

out of the local early tribespeople, the Brigantes, it is a reconstruction of the sort of settlement whose sites we meet all up and down these valleys.

There's a fortified farmstead — a round house with a stone wall, wooden palisade and circular thatched roof, built to house a family of up to a

Replica of cup-and-ring markings at Brigantium. But what did they mean?

dozen — a simulated Bronze Age cairn, and a four-stone circle, based on the one at Three Kings four miles up the valley. There are also replications of the cup-and-ring markings which the ancient folk so frequently and mysteriously carved on handy rocks.

This being round Millennium time there are the usual appurtenances — tea-room, audio-visual display, and a hands-on, inter-active set-up where the kiddies can dig for supposed artefacts in a special excavation tray so long as they re-bury them for the next visitor!

There may not be as much to see as at the older-established showplaces of things Roman, but at least it's a start towards giving some recognition to our other ancestors.

Chapter Five

Redesdale — for Elsdon and Otterburn

Elsdon gibbet or Winter's Stob — a lesson from Baden-Powell

Redesdale's military links continue from the Roman period to the present day, via the Battle of Otterburn, of which more later, to the modern artillery ranges which take up a vast acreage north of Otterburn to the Border.

Roman echoes here too, in the number of NATO troops from all over Europe who, like the Roman foreign legions, come to exercise here.

Redesdale's Roman forts, in the no-man's-land

57

without the wall, were strung out along Dere-street, the road from York, via Corbridge, right up over the Border to the Antonine Wall between Forth and Clyde. It's today's A68, straight as a die for most of its length, up and down over the ridges with their blind summits, no curves at all until you don't expect them, and with a bad record for accidents. The Normans would have followed a similar route, no doubt, before they charged Robert d'Umfraville with the duty of

> "defending it from enemies and wolves with that sword which King William had by his side when he entered Northumberland."

Wolves there may have been; enemies to the Normans there certainly were. Indeed the clans in these valleys were enemies to all comers, known, at least by the powerful merchant-adventurers of Newcastle, who would not employ them, as

> "either by education or nature, not to be of honest conversation; and they commit frequent thefts and other felonys proceeding from such lewde and wicked progenitors."

The word 'blackmail' originated in these parts—another name for the protection money paid by the poorer farmers for the return of a proportion of their lifted stock and/or as insurance against further raids. Yet the villains had their uses. The Duke of Northumberland once wrote to Henry VIII offering to let slip

> "them of Tyndail and Riddisdail for the annoyance of Scotland."

William Grey, author of the early local history *Chorographia* in 1649, wrote how the highlanders

> "come down from these dales into the low countryes, and carry away horses and cattell so cunningly, that it will be hard for any to get them, or their cattell except they be acquainted with some master thiefe; who for some mony (which they call saufey mony) may help them to their stolen goods, or deceive them. There is many every yeare brought in of them into the goals of Newcastle, and at the Assizes are condemned and hanged, sometimes twenty or thirty."

If they escaped the law and fell out among themselves, they took it into their own hands and

> "bang it out bravely, one and his kindred against the other and his; they will subject themselves to no justice, but in an inhumane and barbarous manner, fight and kill one another."

The land is peaceful today, with a soft beauty about it in the mists of the long purple horizons, yet it does not need a great deal of imagination to feel echoes of the ancient violence once what rare sun the area sometimes get goes in. Neither do you need to be an architectural expert to realise that a large number of its farm buildings were once heavily fortified.

Redesdale has two main villages, Elsdon and Otterburn. Elsdon has an ancient motte-and-bailey, a pele tower in the rectory, a church at which St. Cuthbert's wandering body is held to have rested (hence its patronymic), one pub, the

Crown Inn, and the site of the gibbet upon which the body of one William Winter, returned from transportation to his bad old ways, was hung up for the murder of an old woman in 1791.

He had been arrested on information laid by a shepherd boy, who had noticed the unusual pattern of his boot soles, and this example of the power of observation was cited by Baden-Powell in *Scouting For Boys*, a lesson to us all. The wood of the gibbet was reckoned for some time after the body disappeared to be a cure for the toothache. Chewed, presumably. A modern reconstruction of the gibbet stands by the base of a medieval stone cross at the top of an ancient drove road. On a bleak winter's day it is hard not to imagine that it is still in use.

Elsdon is on a tributary of the Rede, and it is a cold spot. An eighteenth-century vicar, the Rev. Charles Dodgson, a man apparently of some wit, and grandfather of Charles Lutwidge Hodgson, aka Lewis Carroll, author of *Alice in Wonderland*, gave a good description of Redesdale in winter while snowed in at Elsdon:

> "There is not a single tree or hedgerow within twelve miles to break the force of the wind; it sweeps down like a deluge from hills capped with everlasting snow, and blasts almost the whole country into one continuous barren desert. The whole country is doing penance in a white sheet...."

And he summed up:

> *"If I was not assured by the best authority upon earth that the world was to be destroyed by fire,*
> *I should conclude that the day of destruction is at hand, but brought on by an agent the very opposite to that of heat."*

Elsdon may be the traditional capital of Redesdale, but Otterburn is bigger, and on the River Rede itself. It is the site of the celebrated Otterburn Mill, which sells its woven blankets, rugs and tweeds all over the world. Queen Victoria had a travelling rug made here.

Less than a mile to the north is the Percy Cross, eight feet high on a medieval base, commemorating the Battle of Otterburn of 1388 which is celebrated in the famous old ballad called Chevy Chase:

> It fell about the Lammas tide,
> When the muir-men win their hay,
> The doughty Douglas bound him to ride
> Into England to drive a prey.
> And he has burned the dales of Tyne,
> And part of Bambroughshire,
> And three good towers on Reidswire fells,
> He left them all on fire.

There are several versions of this ballad, some of which make it appear to have been little more than just another tribal fray. The Scottish version, used by Sir Walter Scott, is an heroic epic, with the two feuding families, Percy of England and Douglas of Scotland, fighting it out to the end by moonlight. Young Percy, Hotspur to his friends and to Shakespeare, takes on the Douglas in single combat:

> When Percy wi' the Douglas met,
> I wat he was fu' fain;

They swakked their swords till sair they swat,
And the blude ran down like rain.

Douglas dies and an exhausted Hotspur is taken prisoner by Sir Hugh Montgomery, Douglas's nephew.

This deed was done at the Otterbourne,
About the breaking of the day;
Earl Douglas was buried at the braken bush,
And the Percy led captive away.

Chevy Chase is one of the finest of the old Border Ballads. Sir Philip Sidney said that it stirred his heart more than a trumpet-call, and Scott is supposed to have lain dying with its words on his lips. If mutual slaughter is ridiculous, then the Borders go from it to the sublime in some of their music and poetry; the ballads so often recording the violence of life, their rhythm and words showing a grim beauty. The historian G.M. Trevelyan, whose family was Northumbrian, wrote of the old balladeers:

"Like the Homeric Greeks, they were cruel, coarse savages, slaying each other as the beasts of the forest; and yet they were also poets who could express in the grand style the inexorable fate of the individual man and woman, and infinite pity for all the cruel things which they nonetheless perpetually inflicted upon one another. It was not one ballad-maker alone but the whole cut-throat population who felt this magnanimous sorrow, and the consoling charm of the highest poetry."

Today, in a grove of trees by the A696 just to the west of Otterburn, not far from the spot where Douglas is supposed to have met his death, stands

The Percy Cross, Otterburn.
Where Harry Percy met his end

the monument which they call the Percy Cross. But then its builders, presumably, would be English.

The common soldiers of both sides would most likely have been buried in mass graves. It could have been one of these that was found when Elsdon Church was restored in 1877, for the remains of over 100 men (no women and no children either) were found buried by the north wall, the skulls of one row neatly tucked into the thigh bones of another to save space.

Chapter Six

Bellingham

The old Station of Redesmouth Junction

Back down Redesdale to the North Tyne again: Redesmouth itself has old British remains in High Countess Park overlooking the main river over a mile from the Rede confluence, and traces of iron-smelting which may go back to prehistory. There is what's left of the station of Redesmouth Junction, where yet another railway line went off eastward up Redesdale, over the moors to split again at Scots Gap for Rothbury to the north and Morpeth to the east. The traveller was often spoilt for choice in those days.

Certainly industry rears its head now in traditional Northumbrian fashion, for there is coal in fair quantity beneath this area; northwards to Bellingham. Not long since a fair-sized slice of Shitlington Common was opencast for coal, and you can still see the scars of older deep-mine workings on the fellside above Bellingham as you approach from the south. Perhaps from the Pennine Way, which, having followed Hadrian's Wall for a dozen miles near the Cumbrian border, sweeps up north-eastwards through the huge

Wark Forest and gets its first sight of the North Tyne after crossing the lovely Warks Burn just east of its confluence at Wark village.

Bellingham itself is the nearest the North Tyne is going to get to a capital. With a population of around 1,000 it still manages to look as it was well advised to look during the old times of trouble—as if it wasn't there at all. Its buildings are nowhere at all high; even the church squats among the houses as if in hiding, and has neither tower nor spire to advertise its presence. Nonetheless it was burned at least twice during the Middle Ages and has a unique stone-slab roof as protection against any further attempts at

Bellingham centre and South African war memorial

arson. It's an old church, originally built around 1200, and dedicated like so many in these parts to St Cuthbert.

Perhaps people were still a little godfearing in its early years, but piety stood little chance of nourishment as time went on. Indeed records in Durham's Dean and Chapter Library show that in 1607 Bellingham's little church did very little custom at all. Holy Communion was given only once a year or so, the font had been smashed, and bibles and prayer books were missing, which perhaps mattered not too much, as it was recorded that such clergy as there were could neither read nor write.

Allowing for a certain amount of exaggeration., it seems that the priesthood was not over-respected in these parts. Percy Reed of Troughend just south of Otterburn, a noted hardcase and one-time Keeper of Redesdale, who came to a sticky end recorded in another well-known ballad, once refused to do penance and pulled his parish priest's beard. But there were exceptions to the general rule. It is, for example, hard to contemplate anyone pulling the beard of the Rev. Bernard Gilpin, rector of Houghton-le-Spring in County Durham, who became known as the Apostle of the North on account of the missionary-like work he did among the turbulent clans along the Border.

Long before the Wesleys were tramping all over the rougher districts spreading the word of what would become Methodism in the most unpromising places, Gilpin would do an annual round of the wildest parts of the northern dales, preaching in a church if there was one, and if not in a barn, or, early-Christian style, out in the open air. He was, as is not unusual when a Man of God is also seen to be a man of the people and willing to get off his backside to get out and

Bellingham Church — a low profile

63

spread the Word, immensely respected. There is little doubt that he would have preached here at Bellingham as well as the churches further south, although there is no evidence to show that it was here that a thief who had taken Mr Gilpin's horses by mistake returned them all of a tremble because, he said, he was fully expecting to be carried off by the Devil as he had carried off the horses.

What is documented in the annals of St Cuthbert's is the time that one John Charlton, known as 'Bowerie' from his living at a place called the Bower up river, killed James Widdrington in a duel over a horse in 1709.

Whether or not as some sort of punishment, the authorities had Widdrington buried in the nave of Bellingham church, just under the door to Charlton's pew, almost literally laying his sin at his doorstep. Bowerie, it is said, never entered the church again.

Outside St Cuthbert's is the well bearing his name, which was held to have miraculous properties. There is also, alongside the northern wall, a curious grave shaped in a long curved hump. It looks — especially if you've heard the story — just like a long, old-fashioned pedlar's pack, and that is what the locals say it commemorates.

St. Cuthbert's Well

Chapter Seven

Bellingham and the Lang Pack

The Lang Pack grave — but who lies beneath?

The legend of the Lang Pack was written up originally by James Hogg, the Ettrick Shepherd, friend of Wordsworth and Scott as well as being a brilliant poet in his own right. The story is supposed to have taken place at Lee Hall, another Charlton house a little to the south of Bellingham, at a time when every man looked out for himself and there really was no such thing as society. The then owner of the hall being away in the South, the house was left in charge of the servants with strict instructions to let no strangers in. Not, I imagine, that they would need in those days to be told such a thing.

Anyway, one evening up turned a pedlar—a good-looking, plausible sort of chap of course — asking for a night's lodging. Disregarding his promising good looks, the young housemaid refused him according to instructions. But she did agree that, to save his trouble, she would let him leave his heavy pack in her charge for the night while he tried his luck elsewhere.

As darkness fell, the girl, growing either restless or bored, thought she would see what was in the pack. Taking a candle to it, and no doubt prodding it a bit, she was more than a little alarmed to see the bundle move. Calling for help from the other servants, she was relieved to find them armed. One lad — we all know the type, don't we? — decided to empty his blunderbuss into the pack to see what would happen. A loud bellow of pain is what happened—that and a gush of blood and then the groans of death. Not sporting, but effective.

Opening up the pack they found a very dead man, evidently sent to open up the premises to his mates during the night, a sort of one-man Trojan horse. He was equipped with a silver whistle which, when someone blew it, summoned the dead man's accomplices. But the servants, forearmed as well as forewarned, gave these such a burst of short-range fire that a number of them were killed. The others got away with the bodies, however, and though a large reward was offered, no one was ever brought to justice. Nor was the man in the long pack ever identified before his burial. What happened to the servant girl or her colleague who fired the first shot is not recorded.

The pedlar, of course, was never seen again, but conjecture still goes on, providing a point of curiosity for tourists and walkers from the Pennine Way who find themselves with the choice of overnighting themselves and their long packs at the youth hostel or at one of the three pubs.

There's not a lot else, except for a neat little heritage centre opened and run by a group of local enthusiasts, and including a fine collection of photographs taken early last century by a Liverpool-born man called Walter Percy Collier who settled in Bellingham around 1912. After serving as an aerial photographer in the First World War he spent the rest of his life running a photographic shop in the centre of the village and chugging round the surrounding countryside on a motor-bike taking photographs of the scenery, the architecture, and the farming activity. These sold well as picture-postcards to be sent home by holidaymakers, who were beginning just then to turn up in increasing numbers. Many of these pictures, which give a fascinating idea of life in and around the North Tyne seventy years ago and more, are on display in a mock-up of Collier's original shop. Others have been published in book form, edited by Stanley Owen, a Birmingham schoolmaster.

Not that the place has changed all that much. There were more people then than you would see around today on the pictures of hay-making and sheep-clipping, and horses rather than tractors. The railway has gone now, and there has been something of a revolution around the topmost end of the valley, and more of that later. But looking at the faces on these old photographs, or at the farmers from miles around who pack the big sheep-fair every August still, it is not hard to imagine that these are the same faces you might have seen round here any time during the past two thousand years; the same names too in many cases.

But surely these can't be the same stock who robbed and pillaged and caused general mayhem and misery as a way of life for so many centuries? Yet look closer. Look, for instance, at the group photograph of Bellingham Football Club, 1919-20 in Collier's collection. Fierce-looking lads these, with determined expressions, for all the cigarettes stuck in their mouths. Fix a steel bonnet on each head and your old-time reivers live again. The leather case-ball in the front of the picture might just as easily be a Scottish head.

Bellingham Football Club 1920 — ancestral faces. From postcard by Walter Collier.

For all its windswept setting, Bellingham has its beauty spots, notably the Hareshaw Linn a mile north and just off the Pennine Way, where the waters plunge over a sandstone cliff nearly 100 feet high into a beautifully wooded ravine full of wych-elm and oak.

Long-pack marauders and Pennine Way walkers come and go, but this, you sense, has been a local promenade for hundreds of years.

Hareshaw Lynn

Chapter Eight
Charlton country and the pele towers

Hesleyside House — elegance in a wild country

By Bellingham the main river takes an almost ninety-degree turn from the lower north-south alignment to go east-west. From now on this will be the Upper North Tyne, another twenty miles to the source and the Scottish Border.

The feel of the countryside does not change dramatically yet—still mile after mile of wide horizons to heather moorland with the ghosts of reivers rampaging all over it. There is, though, one contrast just to the west of Bellingham, at

69

Hesleyside, where a fine mansion stands in lush parkland laid out by Capability Brown in 1778. Hesleyside is the main ancestral home of the Charltons, one of the most powerful of the Border families, and it's still in their hands today.

Like many such, the house was originally a pele tower, but was added to over the centuries, while the Charltons themselves, a noted Old Catholic family, took part in the Pilgrimage of Grace in 1536 against Henry VIII's dissolution of the monasteries, the Battle of Agincourt, and dozens of more local skirmishes, although they were a little quieter during the Jacobite risings of 1715 and 45, which a lot of Catholic families were not.

The hall itself has a fine cantilevered double-staircase by Bonomi (1806), a priest's hole and a private family chapel. There's also the famous 'Spur of the Charltons' which according to legend was served up by the lady of the house whenever times were hard and hungry, as a none-too-subtle hint to the menfolk to get mounted and raid some neighbour's herd and replenish the larder.

In more recent times the Charlton family grew more public-spirited, being great benefactors in Bellingham (the bridge, the workhouse and tramp ward, now the local library), and was one of the prime movers in the building of the North Tyne railway.

Before Hesleyside, the Charltons came from the village on the north side called Charlton, though whether they gave their name to the place or the other way round is not clear. It originally had its own pele tower, since vanished, and a mile or so further upstream is the green mound which once seated Tarset Castle at the junction of the North Tyne and the Tarset Burn. The castle was destroyed in 1525 and never rebuilt.

But it was a formidable enough stronghold at one time, apparently. Eneas Mackenzie, in his *History of Northumberland* early in the nineteenth century, says:

> "Its magnitude, strength and antiquity have combined to impress the minds of the neighbouring people with the notion of its having been the dreadful habitation of a giant."

Legend says that a tunnel ran from Tarset right under the bed of the North Tyne, to Dally Castle, seat of a branch of the Charltons, over a mile away. This might seem a sheer impossibility, like most legends of subterranean passages all over the country, except that we should not forget that the men round these parts were traditionally skilled miners. Local legend also says that rumbling noises used to be heard underground, and carriages emerge from the ground drawn by pairs of headless horses.

Most castles hereabouts started as peles, and developed only if their owners were more ruthlessly successful than their neighbours. A fine example of what an ordinary bog-standard pele looked like can be found by taking a five-mile detour north up the Tarset Burn where, on the edge of the forestry, the Black Middens bastle-house has been opened to the public by English Heritage, complete with outside stone staircase by which occupants could reach their quarters above the cattle, and from which, with any luck, they could drive off raiders. It is possible that this staircase was originally a wooden ladder, easily hauled up for extra safety. There are two more fine peles in the hamlet of Gatehouse nearby.

Many of these towers and bastle-houses were surrounded by an enclosed yard called a barmkin, and an Act of Parliament from 1535 shows that defensive building was not a haphazard process:

> "....every landed man dwelling on or near the Border having land worth £100 a year shall

Black Middens Pele — a borders man's home was his castle

build a barmkin upon his land in a place most convenient and of stone and lime....it should be used by the tenants and their goods in time of strife. If he wishes, the owner can build a tower within the barmkin for his own safety. All other landed gentry of smaller income should build peles and great strengths as they please for the safety and protection of themselves, their tenants and their goods...."

In bad times towers were often in contact with each other, using beacons to warn of thieves' approaches. Neighbourhood Watch? There's nothing new. Neither is intimidation of witnesses just a modern phenomenon. A warning from Sir Robert Bowes in 1551 to victims of theft in Tynedale not to waste their time going to Law went on:

"For if the thief be of any great surname or kindred, and he be lawfully executed by order of the justice, the rest of his kin or surname bear such malice, which they call deadly feud, against such as follow the law against their cousin the thief, as though he had unlawfully killed him with a sword."

Gatehouse Pele — marauders beware boiling water

Chapter Nine

Falstone, Kielder Reservior and Plashetts

Kielder Dam — Falstone Forest in the background

There were towers all the way up North Tynedale, some in the villages which have since disappeared or been incorporated into more recent buildings.

Now the old village of Falstone (two pubs and a tea-room) is dominated by a far bigger structure which towers right over it, and which old-timers would have thought one of the wonders of the world — the dam of the great Kielder Reservoir.

It's the largest man-made lake in Europe, supplying 200 million gallons of water a day to the north-east region. And its site is in the middle of the huge Kielder Forest, biggest acreage of man-made forest in Europe. They haven't done things by halves up here.

The forest came first. The newly-established Forestry Commission started planting in 1920 over the Border near Newcastleton. In 1926 they spread over to start above Falstone, incorporating a large chunk of the Duke of Northumberland's

Kielder Estate in 1932. Now the total Border Forest Park includes Kielder, Wark, Redesdale, and Falstone in Northumberland; Wauchope and Newcastleton forests in Scotland, and Spadeadam in Cumberland, and it covers over 280 square miles of mostly poor upland.

At first mainly Sitka spruce trees were planted, spiky conifers unpleasant to handle and hardly

Winter over Kielder Water

Cruiser 'Osprey' on Kielder Water

prepossessing to look at (when you've seen your first ten million or so sitkas you've really seen the lot). Still around 75 per cent of Kielder is sitka, but there are also Norway spruce (the familiar Christmas tree), Douglas firs and lodgepole pine. Of recent years a more enlightened commission than the early body which planted hideously in straight-edged blocks regardless of hill and valley, has been establishing larger numbers of broad-leaved trees—oak, ash, willow and rowan—partly for the look of things and partly to encourage a more varied wild life.

But then the early Commission planners did not really think of much beyond the economy of commercial timber. Today they welcome visitors and, presumably with the thought in mind that not every member of the public is hell-bent on pinching Christmas trees and setting fire to the rest, they have developed a huge playground.

There are forest trails, picnic-spots, visitor-centres, rough roads for rally drivers and coaxers of husky-dog teams, camp sites, craft centres, sculpture displays, you name it.... When you note that they advertise the whole kit-and-caboodle as 'The Kielder Experience' you'll gather just how present-day public-friendly they've become.

Added to this Experience there is of course the reservoir, or Kielder Water as they now call it to tune in better with the recreational idea. Several times a day the cruiser *Osprey* makes a circuit of the main part of the lake, calling at various viewpoints like Tower Knowe and the Leaplish Waterside Park. At the former there's a visitor centre and an exhibition called *Kielder, the First 500 Million Years*, which may sound ambitious but does not take all that long to get around. Leaplish provides hire facilities for water sports and cycling, and you can play crazy golf (if you

Kielder Water — reservoir or playground?

should have travelled all that way for this sort of Experience). You can water-ski, swim if you've got a cast-iron constitution, fish for all manner of prey, canoe, or peep at the wild life of both lake and forest. One species the authority does not advertise is *nemotocera*, the family which includes the midge.

People from the South are not usually familiar with the midge, confusing it with the harmless gnat. But the Kielder Midge is at least equal in virulence and determination to the disreputable midge of the Scottish Western Highlands and Islands.

It swarms in its millions (or probably thousands of millions: you don't feel like counting after a nip or two) and can make life a misery in summer, particularly a wet or humid summer.

Midges or not, you can visit Kielder Castle, which was never really a castle at all, but a shooting-box belonging to an eighteenth-century Duke of Northumberland, and is now the forest's main visitor centre, where you will have no difficulty in buying the sort of things which are sold these days to centre-visitors. There is even a 'Long Pack' craft shop.

The castle came about in a characteristically sporting manner It was the year 1775, and the Duke sent his son, Earl Percy, to look for a spot where gentlemen could stay when they felt like a spot of shooting wild creatures. Someone's dog went missing chasing a black-cock, and was recovered on a hill where the castle now stands. The owner of the mutt, a Mr Williams,

"was so charmed with the situation that he

summoned the Party to the ground, who all concurred in the Earl's determination to build it there; whereupon a servant was despatched to Hedley's for a bottle of wine, every man drawn up with shouldered musquet, and after a 'success to Kielder Castle' was drank by all under a general discharge, the word of command was given by Governor Williams, (an Honor confer'd in the field on him by his Lordship) and the bottle broke over the butt end of his musquet to mark the spot for laying the foundation, and a cheerful evening concluded a joyous day."

This account, written by Charles Williams, afterwards Governor of the castle, was found in an old game book.

Three quarters of a mile south-east of the castle a huge prehistoric cairn called the Devil's Lapful shows that this remote area has a history older than most. Although it is so often referred to in old guide books as being one of bleakness and desolation, it was not so entirely. In order for the reservoir to be filled quite a number of farms and cottages had to be drowned, as well as entire rows of colliery houses (or what was left of them) at Plashetts, where outcrop coal had been mined for generations.

Plashetts — it's a lovely-sounding name, isn't it, bringing thoughts of bright, tumbling burns and little waterfalls going 'plash'. No doubt this was all so, but Plashetts really meant coal. In 1862 a small drift had been driven by the Belling

Kielder — end of the resevoir and the dam

Burn, north-west of Falstone, but when its coal proved unsatisfactory alternative mines were started a little further to the west above the river and the railway line to which the coal was conveyed down an inclined plane known, after the coal-owner, as Slater's Incline.

This also provided the only route in or out for the population of nearly 300 people housed in straight colliery-type rows with outside netties — a slice of County Durham or Tyneside grafted onto the Border wilderness. This must have been the most isolated industrial settlement in the kingdom, but it had its own school, its own pub, and a flourishing chapel.

The company did quite well for a time, supporting even its own coke-ovens and brickworks. But during the General Strike of 1926 the workings flooded beyond repair. Mr Slater the owner went into the drift to assess the damage, but was overcome by gas and consequently died of it. The colliery practically died with him, and the community was not long in following suit.

Attempts were made to resume coal-winning, but by 1932 the little school had only five pupils as against over 100 in its heyday. It was closed and the deserted village was finally demolished in 1952. Today most of this site of a brief period of activity lies beneath the waters of the reservoir. It is as if Plashetts Colliery had never been.

Chapter Ten

Kielder Forest

Kielder Viaduct — Victorian skew-bridge — but where have all the trains gone?

Economically, however, not all was lost with the closure of Plashetts Colliery, for it coincided with the spread of the new forest No doubt some of the workforce turned to timber-planting, and to building the roads which were needed to handle new plant, and hundreds of unemployed men from Tyneside were drafted in and housed in army-style camps nearby. And a new village entirely sprung up around Kielder Castle to house the more permanent forestry workers.

Trees take a long time to grow, and the amount of employment originally foreseen never fully materialised, but in 1976 work began on a dam 170 feet high overlooking Falstone village. At the peak of reservoir construction work 1,500 men, mostly from outside the valley, were employed, but in this wet climate the water soon began to take over, and the scheme was officially opened by Queen Elizabeth in 1982.

It cost £167 million in cash and an untold amount of disruption to the farms and hamlets soon flooded by the gathering waters. Whickhope, Emmethaugh, Otterstone Lee, Wellhaugh, Lewisburn, Gowanburn and Bewshaugh — all flattened and then drowned, and today the pleasure-trippers and small yachtsmen from the towns sail high above them. It is an ill wind that blows nobody any good, but try telling that to a dispossessed farmer whose family has worked a lonely valley hard for generations.

The railway of course had disappeared back in 1956. Stretches of it now give routes to mountain bikers and ramblers, but the only notable sign that it ever served this area at all is the wonderful Kielder Viaduct which still stands near the upper end of the reservoir; the road it once crossed now a stream draining into the lake. It's a skew bridge of seven arches, and its peculiar angle of construction meant that the place and shape of every stone had to be individually calculated. It is of no use today except as a monument to the Victorians' ingenuity and optimism.

But how short-sighted the planners have been more recently. The Kielder Scheme, as well as sending out thousands of tons of timber today,

pulls in thousands of visitors every year, most of whom have to travel nearly forty miles of narrow, twisty road from Hexham, and then the rest from and to their own homes. Cars and motor-coaches compete with caravans and heavy lorries loaded with Kielder timber, and there are very few stretches where it is safe to overtake. It may be an improvement on what between the wars was little more than a glorified farm-track with sixteen gates across it between Hexham and the Border, but it is by no means up to modern requirements.

I am not suggesting that the railway line could somehow have been floated across the reservoir to get right up to Kielder and beyond, but Falstone would have provided a reasonable terminus. Schemes have been mooted for reinstating at least some of the line, but at the time of writing (2002) nothing definite has materialised.

More positive news, however, has come from the village of Kielder itself. Helped by a local council grant, but largely through self-help, the filling-station has been reopened, and the school has taken on a new lease of life by incorporating a community centre, a doctors' surgery, a library and a 40-bed youth hostel. Kielder people have fought back trends and won themselves a new lease of life.

Although around Kielder itself the old railway route has largely vanished beneath forest and water, long stretches of its course can still be seen as you drive north from the forest to the Border at the little hamlet and one-time railway halt at Deadwater. This area is the source of

Kielder Dam

another ballad, this one concerning the fate of the Cowt (Colt) of Kielder, legendary head lad of one of the older families round here, and a giant of a man physically.

The Cowt was invited over to grim Hermitage Castle in Liddesdale by the notorious Lord Soulis, a man renowned for his wickedness. The visit may have seemed foolhardy, but the Cowt

was geared out with magic armour, which came in handy when Soulis turned nasty.

> In my plume is seen the holly green
> With leaves of the rowan tree;
> And my casque of sand by a mermaid's hand
> Was formed beneath the sea.

The magic, however, was not immune to the

81

power of running water, and when Soulis pursues him from Hermitage, Kielder stumbles when crossing the Bells Burn within sight of home, and his enemies fall on him and hold his head under water with their spears until he drowns.

The celebrated Kielder Stone, 1,200 feet up on Peel Fell, is supposed to mark the spot were the Cowt crossed the Scottish Border on his ill-fated journey. It is considered extremely unlucky to go round this rock three times widdershins, or anti-clockwise, though why anyone should want to do this after a rough, five-mile, uphill hike from Kielder escapes me.

Lord Soulis, incidentally, eventually got his come-uppance, being boiled alive in a cauldron of molten lead; his Hermitage stronghold is alleged to have sunk a full foot into the ground with the sheer weight of Soulis's sins.

Deadwater marks the source of the North Tyne. Not an inspiring name, perhaps, and not a particularly inspiring sight. But then few river sources are.

A forest road leads along the Deadwater Burn which is itself quite unspectacular, losing itself in a bog. But lift up your eyes above the legions of conifers to the wild and windy uplands of the Anglo-Scottish watershed over which the old reivers rode on their blood-feuds or cattle-drives, and armies from both England and Scotland used for invasion. They have seen thousands of years of man's changing ambitions and look as unmoved as they ever were almost since time began.

Part Three — The Combined Tynes

Chapter One

Two different worlds

Rural life meets industry

The main dilemma in writing about the River Tyne proper — the unified waters of both North and South Tynes down through Newcastle to the coast — is its sheer size and complexity. The two tributary rivers flowing respectively from the Scottish Border and the Cumbrian fells can be observed, experienced, even walked, fairly simply. Neither is ever very wide, and the country is usually of a piece whichever side you are on; its history much the same on left bank or right. But once you get downstream of Hexham you can be in two different worlds — north or south of the water.

For a start there are, for a large part of this journey, different local authorities involved. Whereas all of the North Tyne and most of the South are in Northumberland, as the combined Tyne gets nearer the sea you have, as well as the ancient divisions between Northumberland and Durham, Newcastle City, Gateshead Metropolitan Borough, North Tyneside and the South Tyneside Metropolitan Borough. Once there was also the conglomerate body known as Tyne and Wear which has now been replaced.

The old territories north and south of the river were historically quite different, and the distinction can still be felt today — from the lands of the Prince Bishops to the fiefdoms of the old border barons and the rich industrialists of the city of Newcastle.

Immense changes are now taking place both in the look and feel of the whole region. It has always been changing of course, but the process seems to be accelerating: as traditional industry folds and collapses, there arrives a host of lighter concerns. As the coal industry dies, as shipyards and engineering works decline, we have a plethora of light industrial and business parks,

and the quality of housing has changed — in some places out of all recognition. Riverside sites which were not so long ago slums or semi-slums have now been cleared and replaced by well-designed but extremely expensive properties. As the working class has been priced or just prised out, the Yuppies have moved in.

And there now seems to be a greater awareness of the environment — a re-awakening of the fierce local pride which was never far from the surface. There is still a great deal of ugliness, or plain dreariness, but people can now enjoy new pedestrian and cycle routes which once were closed to all but those concerned with particular industries and firms.

History has a newly-raised profile, with sites which were once nearly obliterated by industry now being vitalised as visitor attractions. There's a new unity too. Gateshead was for so long a poor relation of Newcastle, but now, especially since the wonderful new 'Winking Eye' pedestrian bridge linking the two, they have drawn closer in a friendly rivalry, linking in a smaller way like Buda and Pest, London and Lambeth.

It is significant that Newcastle teamed up with Gateshead for a joint bid, geared to compete jointly for the title City of Culture in 2008, even if they did not win after being marked favourites.

Chapter Two

Hexham — The Capital of Tynedale

Hexham Abbey — built by the Saxons, spoiled by the Victorians

But back to the rural scene for the start. The twin Tynes, having met beneath Warden Hill with its ancient British fort, the united river is soon at Hexham, ancient capital of Tynedale. Now most settlements along both North and South Tynes owed their proper existence to the Romans, but although the Imperial armies serving the Wall undoubtedly had much to do with the Hexham area, they can hardly be said to have founded the town itself. True there are some priceless Roman carvings and monuments preserved in the Abbey, but these seem to have come originally from Corbridge, which certainly was a most important Roman stronghold.

Prehistoric man had lived all over this area, but Hexham's great days seem effectively to have started with the Saxons. In the Sixth Century, with the Romans just away, leaving a depressed and vulnerable borderland behind them, Christianity made its first, and some would say its greatest, inroads in the North. St. Columba had spread the Gospel from Iona, and St Augustine, sent from Rome, had become the first Archbishop of Canterbury. Then in 625 or so Edwin, Saxon king of Northumbria, converted, and ten years later his son Oswald, saint and martyr as well as king, called in Ionan missionaries under St Aidan, who founded a

Hexham Manor Office — once a gaol, now a museum

monastery at Lindisfarne off the Northumbrian coast. This later became the home of the great St Cuthbert, but first it produced St Wilfrid, who was really the founder of Hexham.

Wilfrid the Benedictine was the man chiefly responsible for the victory at the Synod of Whitby in 664 A.D. of the Roman faction over the old Celtic persuasion. He was a learned, proud, perhaps arrogant and certainly courageous man, and it was he who, between 674 and 678, built at Hexham the monastic church of St Andrew, the finest, they said, of any church this side of the Alps. It swiftly became a cathedral, and although demoted to abbey status during the Danish raids, has dominated the town ever since.

This is not the place to attempt to describe the architectural history of Hexham Abbey — there are plenty of good guides for that — and of course the little original Saxon building has now all but disappeared. The original crypt is still there, but the present main building which rises above the market place has been the work of many centuries including, unfortunately, the nineteenth, when the well-meaning Victorians enlarged and all but ruined the look of the place. But they could not destroy its best features — the spectacular night stairs down which the monks would process to their devotions, and the wonderful carvings of the Choir. Hexham Abbey grew no fewer than seven saints among its early bishops — surely some sort of record.

Hexham may have been a great centre for piety, but being where it was when it was, it could hardly escape the bloodshed and horror which engulfed all this area right down the middle centuries. The Danes raided in the Ninth Century, burned both church and its growing little town, and butchered its people. In 1296 the Scots invaded Northumberland and destroyed the abbey which had only just been restored, and they burned the town again, out-doing the Danes in sheer cruelty by burning to death, it's said, 200 pupils in the main school. What little they left intact was destroyed the following year by another Scottish invasion force in the early years of their War of Independence, after William Wallace harried the defeated English from Stirling right down into their own lands.

For years the tide of Border trouble washed back and forth over Hexhamshire. In 1464 it was the scene of a Yorkist victory over the Lancastrians during the Wars of the Roses, and in 1536 it saw the beginnings of the Pilgrimage of Grace in resistance to Henry VIII's dissolution of the monasteries. This got the Hexham monks nowhere, and their lands and properties were divided among some of the bigger, apparently more loyal families in the Dale. Among them were the Beaumonts, later to be the leading lights in the area.

The story goes that after the Battle of Hexham Levels in 1464, which saw the finish of the Lancastrian cause, Queen Margaret (of Anjou) sought escape after Henry Beaufort, Duke of

Hexham back street — more traditional than the front

Somerset, was beheaded in Hexham Market Place. She was captured by a band of robbers but managed to get away from them while they were quarrelling over her jewels. She then met another outlaw called Black Jack (this story grows more and more improbable) who, on finding she was a queen, hid her and her infant son Edward in a cave in the woods of the Dipton Burn. After two days the queen headed with her son for safety in Scotland and afterwards the

Hexham shambles in the Market Place

(although the smaller shops are often grumbling about the spread of charity establishments), and a growth of tourism. The name of Beaumont, far from being resented, is commemorated in the name of the street before the abbey, where it is topped by a fine statue whose site in the middle of a crossroads a traffic cop might envy. It celebrates a local officer killed during the South African War. Lieutenant-colonel George Elliott Benson appears at first sight to be throwing a pair of binoculars in the face of the enemy, but history records no such last-ditch act of defiance.

Two other buildings in the centre speak of Hexham's turbulent past and of its importance as an administrative centre. The Moot Hall is more of a castle keep than merely the meeting place its name suggests. It was built around 1400 and has a very defensive look. There is a covered barbican, castle-like, guarded by twin towers and projecting stonework from which molten lead, boiling water or anything damagingly handy could be poured or dropped on the heads of attackers, though there is no record I can find of any major siege. It may or may never have been an actual castle, but until 1838 it was a court-house and today houses a museum and art gallery.

so-called Queen's Cave became a favourite local beauty-spot, half a mile or so south of the Racecourse.

There was trouble of a rather different kind in 1761 when a crowd demonstrating against new methods of recruiting for the militia was gunned down in the Market Place by men of the North York Militia. Two soldiers were killed and, after a magistrate gave the order to fire, some fifty civilians as well. Over 300 people were wounded. Afterwards Hexham seems to have settled down to the peaceful sort of life it continues to this day except on the odd Saturday night. There is little industry, some commerce

Another castle-like structure nearby — a square tower like a keep, was called the Manor Office. At one time it was just that, its clerks safe behind walls ten feet thick; at others it was Hexham's own gaol, with dungeons deep beneath.

Today it serves as a museum of the Border counties. Unfortunately the narrow lanes which must have formed a maze around these official buildings have been mostly demolished, and the area has no real identity, neither a proper street nor a decent car park.

Not that central Hexham has lost all its old character. The Market Place still has its covered shambles, built in 1766 soon after the riot, and it is still very much in use today, as colourful and noisy as any open-air bazaar in the North. A narrow lanes system behind it reveals a number of shops rather more interesting than the mere antique-dealers you might expect to have taken over a place like this. There are workshops here — furniture-makers, bicycle-repairers, a cobbler, clock-makers. You get a taste of what a town centre like this was like in the old days when people made things on the spot as well as trying to sell them.

Hexham's most interesting streets are hidden

89

Hexham has liked to refer to itself as the Heart of all England, and one of its many pubs bears that name. Just recently little Haltwhistle a few miles up-river has contested the description, which I should have thought was either meaningless or downright false. Centre of Britain perhaps, if these things are calculated by all-round distance from the sea, but not England. Both towns all but bang their heads on Scotland. I had always believed that the actual English centre—the place which would balance on the point of a pin if the map outline was cut out—was Kenilworth in Warwickshire. But what about islands like the Scillies and Lundy? As if any of it mattered.

There is evidently money around Hexham—landed money, tweedy money, red-faced, burly, pipe-smoking cash. Hexham is the centre of the richest slice of farm-land in South Northumberland if not the whole county. There's arable land round about in contrast to the sheep-rearing uplands, and there is fruit-growing too. The place sees more four-wheeled drives than old bangers, and the charity shops sell some pretty classy cast-offs.

Hexham is short of car-parking space—a good reason for visiting by train before they start talking again about closing its line to Newcastle and Carlisle. The only sure-fire parking area is down the steep Hallstile Bank behind the Moot Hall and in front of a supermarket and leisure centre. If you move a little further out, towards the 1793 bridge over the Tyne, you get a full impression of the town which shows all its contradictions. Uphill the centre and the Abbey, a hilltop town almost Italian except for its greyness. But what sticks out most prominently is the red-brick butt-end of a 'tween-wars cinema, the Forum, now a Wetherspoons pub (somewhat resented by the other pubs for selling food and drink more cheaply and possibly more efficiently).

Alongside the river is Tyne Green, handy for dog-walking, courting, canoeing and picnicking, if necessary all at once, and close by is the new farmers' mart in the middle of a light industrial estate which contains what modern parlance calls a 'civic amenity centre', or garbage-dump in English. To the east a white plume of vapour marks a big chip-board factory which, if you did not know of the town's older attractions, might lead you to believe you were approaching some busy industrial town somewhere in old-time Teeside or East Lancashire.

There you are then: Hexham, which would no doubt claim to have something for everyone, There is 'culture' at the Queen's Hall—a small theatre, cinema, gallery and light eaterie; there's a beautiful horse-racing course above and some three miles from the town from which you can see all over the Shire, and there is as good a selection of pubs and fish-and-chip shops as you would find in any place of the same size. What more could anyone want?

Chapter Three

Corbridge and the Shire

Beaufront Castle — architectural class

If you want a fuller idea of the social status of the Hexham area, just look northward over the river, the railway and the A69, to the spread of hilltop parkland which marks Beaufront Castle and the adjoining Sandhoe Hall. Still further east is Stagshaw House below Stagshaw Bank, where the North's biggest agricultural fairs were held from time immemorial until 1926.

None of these noble piles is particularly old, but who needs age if they've got class? In fact

Beaufront, built in the nineteenth century, stands on the site of an older stately home from Elizabethan times.

Like neighbouring Sandhoe, it was designed by John Dobson, the great architect of nineteenth century Newcastle, and Pevsner calls it:

> "an extremely ambitious enterprise in 'domestic castellated'style, a free mixture of Perpendicular and Tudor Gothic."

It was associated with the ill-fated Earls of Derwentwater, who died in the Jacobite cause. Outlawed, one is said to have hidden in a priest's hole under a staircase at Beaufront. The Derwentwaters belonged to Dilston Hall over on the south side of the Tyne, but before we meet them we shall carry on along the north bank to the settlement of Corbridge, which the Romans called Corstopitum.

This was one of the chain of forts ordered by Julius Agricola some forty years before Hadrian started the Wall. It was strategically important in standing where Dere Street, the road from York and the South, the present-day A68, crossed the Tyne. The town which grew up around it was the most northerly in the whole Roman Empire.

Corbridge Church — Saxon tower, Victorian gateway: not a good match

But again, like neighbouring Hexham, Corbridge's most enduring interest lies in its Saxon past, if only for one building—its beautiful Church of St Andrew (note name same as Hexham's, and we shall meet more). It was built, as was usual in these parts, of stones robbed or 'borrowed' from Roman Corstopitum. Its most remarkable feature is its tall Saxon tower at the west end, and there are further early remains in the walls of the nave. Its early years spanned times of great trouble; both Danes and Scots were here intent on destruction, and traces of fire can still be seen today. Presumably because of the amount of re-building needed over the years, none of the principal walls is at right angles to its neighbour, but it has to be said that unlike other churches of comparable age it has survived the centuries well, not having been well-meaningly vandalised by 'improvers' in more recent times.

There is a twelfth-century pele tower in the churchyard — the 'vicar's pele' — evidence of continuing troubles in the Middle Ages. Modern Corbridge's chief claim to fame seems to be that it was once lived in by the romantic novelist Catherine Cookson, Tyne Dock-born but well-loved in this rather more up-market environment. There is another, larger, pele tower down the east end of the town and it is now lived in privately.

Corbridge itself is built in a triangular pattern, its three main old streets leading to the head of a fine seventeenth-century bridge over the Tyne. This was built in 1674, the only bridge along the whole length of the Tyne not washed

Corbridge, the vicar's pele. Safety for the Parson.

93

away or even damaged by the great winter flood of 1771.

The local story is that the water rose so high that Corbridge folk could wash their hands in the river over the parapet, though one wonders if many of them bothered after what the Rev. John Hodgson, historian, wrote of them in 1807. The place was dirty, he reported, filthy with middens and pigsties.

> "The population seem half fed; the women sallow, thin-armed, and the men flabby, pot-bellied, and tender-footed...."

Not the sort of picture which Corbridge would like to present today, now that it is much favoured by better-off Newcastle commuters seeking one tender foot at least in the country. It is only twenty minutes drive on the A69 into the city (other traffic willing), and even less by the frequent trains. Pigsties and middens indeed!

There are some fine walks around Corbridge: past the excavated Roman fort for one, and out northwards to Aydon and Halton castles, both fine examples of medieval strength.

But perhaps the finest is along the river haugh back westward towards Hexham, to Dilston, and the story of the Derwentwaters.

Corbridge — only survivor of the Great Flood of 1771

Chapter Four

Dilston and the Jacobites

Dilston Castle

James Radcliffe, third and last Earl of Derwentwater, was a cousin of James Stuart, the Old Pretender. As a young man he had inherited Dilston Castle on the Devil's Water, and apparently became well regarded for his hospitality and for his kindness to his tenants.

Perhaps he could well afford both, for he had inherited vast estates, including the wealth of the many lead mines on Alston Moor at the head of the South Tyne. Not that great wealth made many similarly rich men charitable in those days any more than these, but the Rev. Robert Patten wrote of young James:

> "he was a man formed by nature to be generally beloved; and he had a beneficence so universal that he seemed to live for others."

He was to die for others too, as things turned out. When the revolt in support of James Stuart broke out in October, 1715, Radcliffe, a strong Catholic, rode out to Beaufront Castle to join other gentry of the Faith. The rebels rode through Corbridge with drawn swords, raised the Stuart banner at Warkworth up on the coast, and proclaimed the Pretender King of England. They seem to have spent several days riding round the Northumbrian countryside trying to decide on an attack on Newcastle, but the city blocked its gates, recruited hundreds of reinforcements, and so the Jacobites moved over to Hexham, where they again proclaimed King James III in the Market Place, then by way of Kelso and other Border towns, to Preston in Lancashire, having defeated a royalist force at Penrith en route. But King George's troops were in strong pursuit, and the rebels began melting away.

Finally the remnants surrendered without another fight. Derwentwater and his brother Charles were among the leading gentry taken prisoner. The young earl was beheaded on Tower Hill, and although brother Charles escaped to France, he returned to take part in the second Jacobite Rebellion of 1745 and met a similar fate. The Derwentwater estates were forfeited and went to the Greenwich Hospital Commissioners, controllers of the British lighthouse system and similar matters nautical.

The Radcliffe brothers were in the way of becoming martyrs: James' body was removed from its London grave, secretly carried to Northumberland, and re-buried at Dilston. Over a century later, following the morbid curiosity of the time, the coffin was dug up again, the body, they said, found in a state of complete preservation, and a local blacksmith made a tidy sum drawing the noble teeth and selling them for half-a-crown a molar. Brother Charles, thirty years later, had his heart put in a casket, and that too was buried at Dilston.

But was young Radcliffe such a hero as his supporters made out? There are stories that before the first rising he frequently hid from the authorities, and that he only joined the rebels after being taunted by his young wife Anna, who offered him her fan in exchange for his sword so that she could do the fighting instead.

This is probably a vile calumny, for the Radcliffes enjoyed posthumous support for many years. As recently as 1883 a stone roadside cross was put up near Langley to the south of Haydon Bridge, commemorating the brothers *"for their loyalty to their lawful sovereign"*. It still stands today, and whenever the aurora borealis is seen around Dilston, as it was on the night of the first execution, the locals call it 'Lord Derwentwater's Lights'. Or so says Mr William Tomlinson in his celebrated Victorian *Guide to Northumberland.*

Today a few remains of old Dilston Castle still stand above the Devil's Water among fine old trees. There's a bit of a fifteenth-century tower and a Tudor-period doorway. More complete is the chapel next door, one of the very few post-Reformation Catholic chapels in the country, and still with its roof. Nearby is Dilston Hall, now a training college run by the MENCAP charity, and the high, single-arched bridge over the stream. And that's the end of another colourful saga. Dilston Hall can be visited by arrangement with the college.

Chapter Five

Bywell

Bywell St. Peter's

Staying on the south bank of the Tyne, the old Roman Dere Street follows it with the Newcastle-Carlisle railway line between the two down to Riding Mill and Broomhaugh, pretty enough but without a lot of interest except as a 'good' rural address for commuters to and from industrial or, more likely these days, commercial, Tyneside. Three miles further downstream is Stocksfield, and that is much the same, except that it has a bridge, the first since Corbridge, over which you can get to Bywell village, and that, as they say in the vernacular, is something else.

A century ago Bywell gave Mr Tomlinson opportunity for one of his purplest of prose patches.

"A lovely patch of Arcadia preserved to the modern world amid all the industrial changes that have transformed some of the fairest scenes in Northumberland into black and hideous wastes—the retreat of the old doomed divinities of wood and fountain, banished from their native haunts."

Bywell has two churches which on closer examination of the place may seem more than a trifle excessive, for they are about all there is of the village if you except a ruined castle, a vicarage, and the hall which is the home and headquarters of the Beaumont family, lords of Allendale, and that stands in its own acres, removed from the road. There is the White Church and the Black Church. The white is another named after St Andrew, again built by Wilfrid of Hexham, and the black is dedicated to St Peter.

Local legend used to have it that the two churches were built so close to each other because of a quarrel between two sisters, but as there is a century between their building, although both are pre-Norman, this is unlikely to be so. St Andrew's is white because it was run by Premonstratensian or White Canons, and St Peter's by the Benedictines, whose habit is black. St Peter's is the parish church of Stocksfield; St Andrew's of the township of Styford and points west.

Big names were here way back: both the Baliols

and the Nevilles ran Bywell at different times before, each in his own way, being dispossessed for treason. Before them there was a settlement on the south side of the river where a round hill is reckoned to have been a moot or meeting-place for the local elders.

This may all be interesting historically, and as an extreme example of the vagaries of more recent Anglican organisation, but what hits the visitor hardest is the emptiness of the place. It's beautifully green and well-tree'd today, but once this was a thriving community. There were 500 or so people living here in the Middle Ages, with fifteen workshops, mostly run by craftsmen in iron, who would make weapons, bits of harness, farm tools and wrought decoration for buildings. They were skilled bowmen too, and you can see where they would sharpen their arrows on the church stonework after Mass, to keep them,

"stoute and hardy by contynuall practyse."

Bywell suffered from raids like all the villages in Tynedale, when the cattle would be herded for safety into the main street between the churches. It was also badly hit by the great flood of 1771 when six people drowned, ten houses were washed away, and a baby girl still alive and well in her wooden cradle was found floating near the mouth of the Tyne some thirty miles away. But another story goes that the emptiness is due to a wholesale clearance of the village by the Beaumont family in the nineteenth century. They wanted the place to themselves and so settled the people out of sight in Stocksfield over on the other side of the river. All, that is, but the

Bywell St. Andrew's

vicar of St Andrew's. He refused to go, so the Hall had a high wall built to shut off sight and sound of him. Some people still speak of it as the 'spite wall' today.

We are fortunate in this part of the world to have such places as Bywell. We may take its beauty and its rich history for granted, but we should remind ourselves that the Americans would probably give a fortune if they could dig the whole place up and transport it sod by sod to Minnesota or Iowa, and perhaps we ought to keep our fingers crossed, for stranger things have happened in transatlantic relations

From Stocksfield eastward the southern bank of the Tyne begins to get quite built up, but if we stay on the north side things are still quite rural almost to the outskirts of Newcastle. After Bywell, and both between the A69 and the river are the twin villages of Ovington and Ovingham. They are similar only in name.

Ovington

Ovingham

Chapter Six

Two great natives — Stephenson and Bewick

Ovingham St. Mary's — yet another Saxon Tower

Enthusiasts for Saxon church architecture could round off a good day's catch in Tynedale by visiting St Mary the Virgin at Ovingham. It completes the set from Warden at the twin Tynes' confluence, via Hexham Abbey, to Corbridge and Bywell St Andrew's. Like them it made free use of stone from Hadrian's Wall, and like them has a particularly impressive tower, in this case the highest pre-Conquest example on the Tyne. Its narrow windows indicate that it was built as much for defence as for piety, and indeed it was the scene of one of the few instances of clerical resistance to the Dissolution of the Monasteries, when the priest-in-charge of its Augustinian cell, the self-styled 'Master of Ovingham', greeted Henry's Commissioners with a drawn longbow, swearing that he would die before he gave up the house. Whether he did or not we don't know, but we would, presumably, if he had.

It was in the porchway of Ovingham Church that perhaps the greatest of all British wood-engravers, Thomas Bewick, 1753-1828, practised his art as a child, covering its floor with chalk drawings.

> "At that time I had never heard of the word 'drawing'." he records in his fine Memoir, "Nor did I know of any other paintings besides the king's arms in the church, and the signs in Ovingham of the Black Bull, the White Horse, the Salmon and the Hounds and Hare. I always thought I could make a better hunting scene than the latter; the others were beyond my hand."

Another time, he relates, he was locked in the same church as a punishment.

> "This solitary confinement was very irksome to me, as I had not at that time got over a belief in ghosts and boggles for the sight of which I was constantly on the lookout. Oppressed with fear I peeped here and there into every corner, in dread of seeing some terrible spirit."

A typical engraving by Bewick

After a while, though, young Bewick tired of this and passed his time shinning up the columns and perching on their capitals.

And he soon developed his artistic skill, setting up in Newcastle near the cathedral and producing wonderful engravings in miniature, mostly of rural subjects, including those for his History of Quadrupeds and the twin volumes of 'British Birds' (1797 and 1804). They buried Bewick in Ovingham churchyard, opposite his birthplace at Cherryburn House across the river at Mickley, now a fine museum. There is also a stone slab to his memory in the church porch where he developed his art as a child.

A famous contemporary of Bewick's — another local genius — was born just three miles down-river at Wylam. George Stephenson came from High Street House, a red-tiled cottage

Cherryburn House — birthplace of Thomas Bewick

standing appropriately right beside a stretch of the railway of which, by most consent these days, he was the father. Perhaps this place of birth and his inventiveness were not a coincidence, for the line, now disused, ran along the old Wylam Waggonway, a wooden-railed system for hauling coals from the nearby colliery to Lemington, where they were transferred to lighters on the river. It would have been young Stephenson's earliest outlook, and he would walk along it, between the horse-drawn wagons, to visit his father at work in the engine-house at the pit.

Young George was to follow family by becoming a fireman at Wylam Colliery, before moving to Killingworth where he invented his first safety-lamp, the 'Geordie'. He was awarded £1,000 for this invention, a large sum for a young working man in those days, but his more lasting fame rests on his improvements to both steam engines and railway track which he developed while working at Killingworth. Stephenson's trackside birthplace, with its plaque showing the famous Rocket, is now another museum and tea-room run by the National Trust and open in summer-time.

Past it now runs a cycle track along which you can ride right through Newcastle to Wallsend and another museum, which celebrates his work in steam, near Killingworth. Soon, it is hoped, the track will go right through to the coast at Tynemouth.

Another famous birthplace — Stephenson's cottage at Wylam

Chapter Seven

Prudhoe and the beginnings of industry

Prudhoe Castle — but where did the Umfravilles get to?

The connections here at Wylam with the great engineer are a reminder that industrial Tyneside is not far away, and there were iron foundries at Wylam itself way back. But there are yet traces of the old rural, feudal past over at Prudhoe.

It is now an industrial town in its own right, with Kimberly-Clark's paper factory, but it has a long history too, centred on the Norman castle on a scarped ridge above the Tyne. This is mostly in ruins, but its keep, with its tall turret, can be seen from miles around.

Prudhoe was the seat of the Umfraville family, one of the most powerful in the feudal North, having been bestowed by William himself. Although a later Umfraville fell out for a while with King John, the family seems to have kept the castle for the best part of 300 years; Odonel de Umfraville holding out there against William the Lion in a three-day siege after the Scottish king had already sacked several other Northumbrian strongholds and made a mess of Carlisle. One is inclined to wonder what happened to the Umfravilles. Theirs is not a name you come across every day, and you would look for it in vain in the local telephone directories.

Probably they just died out: Countess Maud, widow of the last feudal baron at Prudhoe, married into the Percy family, earls and dukes of Northumberland, who passed on the ruin quite

Ryton Willows — beauty-spot at dusk

recently to English Heritage. Or perhaps the Umfravilles just went ex-directory.

Until a few years ago this was all coal country. The Durham county boundary is near, and up in this high corner the coal seams thrust up and cropped out near the surface, resulting in dozens (probably hundreds over the years) of small pits. The deeper, thicker seams, and therefore the more productive collieries, were found nearer the coast and were mostly sunk more recently as powerful machinery became available. Small matter now perhaps, for there is not one of any size left working, and a new generation of young marrieds has grown up, buying new houses in commuter villages on both sides of the Tyne, who might not even be aware that their new bijou address was once part of a pit village.

Still on the south side of the Tyne, Prudhoe gives way to West Wylam, which lost its pit quite early (I remember covering its closure for the *Evening Chronicle* back in 1958), and then there's Crawcrook, where they produce, for reasons best known to themselves, immense numbers of Christmas turkeys. Then there's Ryton, with its own little beauty-spot at Ryton Willows.

Ryton is now part of an enlarged Gateshead, the Metropolitan Borough Council which extends over a large part of what, historically, belonged to the Prince Bishopric of Durham. "*Welcome*," it says on a roadside sign today, "t*o Gateshead, home of the 1990 Garden Festival.*" Memories are long around here.

And now you're in sight of Stella. Now anywhere else in Britain Stella would have been

Stella — what's left of the power station

a little beauty-spot, a picnic-place maybe, feminine with flower-beds and shrubs to match its dainty name.

On Tyneside it had to be a power-station, and until recently its massive chimneys and cooling-towers effectively marked the start of industrial Tyneside.

Stella itself has shrunk to a sprawling electricity sub-station, full of the paraphernalia of power and looking rather like the innards of an old-time wireless set built for a giant, its pylons and supply-lines marching out to all points of the compass.

Now, for nearly twenty miles yet, is what used to be the most varied, most inventive, busiest, dirtiest, noisiest concentration of factories in all the North, mixed up with the houses and tenements of the people who worked them when they could, and the shops, offices, churches, chapels and supporting institutions that served them all. Today things are not quite the same.

But I jump ahead. We're still around Stella and what used to be its power station, ready to hold breath and move into Tyne proper — the Tyne, the Tyne, the Coaly Tyne, Queen of all the Rivers.

That's what they used to chant anyway, wherever a few Geordies got together. Now they'll just shout of 'the Toon' or some such mantra about their football club. Perhaps it's all much the same.

There were collieries around Stella and Ryton, sunk way back in the seventeenth century, and most productive on the river for their time. Stella and Swalwell were also busy passing on the smelted lead from the high fells to ships on the river. And there were lead refineries at Blaydon, which was to become famous in song with the Geordies' 'national anthem', *The Blaydon Races*. This celebrates, for no reason that most people can work out, a disastrous outing to the race-meeting near Stella via Newcastle's Scotswood road, with;

> Aal the lads an' lasses there,
> Aal wi' smilin' faces,
> Gannin' alang the Scotswood Road,
> Te see the Blaydon Races.

Dunston coal staiths — once the start of the oldest sea-journey in Britain

The song was really a lively slice of self-advertisement by a music-hall singer called George Ridley, and ends with the exhortation to

gan' an' see Geordie Ridley's show,
At the Mechanics' Hall in Blaydon.

Because by then (1862) the Blaydon district was an industrial centre in its own right, with the Derwent tributary joining the Tyne, a busy place indeed for the shipping of raw materials.

Swords were forged at Shotley Bridge up-stream by German ex-pats; next door was Winlaton with the huge ironworks of Ambrose Cowley, a Greenwich ironmonger who had imported workers from Liege in Belgium.

There was ample charcoal for smelting, the waters of Derwent for tempering, and a ready dispatch-port for ships to London down the Tyne, which was navigable then twenty miles from the sea. Until quite recently the coal staithes at Dunston were the start of regular sailings by the little flat-bottomed colliers which could negotiate the Thames bridges en route for the metropolitan power stations.

'Sea coal' they had called London's fuel, and its transport down the east coast must have been the oldest regular industrial journey in Britain. All gone now in a few short years of destruction, many of the great wooden coal-jetties — the staiths in local parlance — with it. Those that remain are part of a marina for pleasure-boats.

Crowley was a benevolent employer, to rank alongside Robert Owen of New Lanark nearly a century later. He housed his workers decently, there was insurance against sickness, old age and death, and a company doctor, schoolmaster and a clergyman employed on the workers' behalf, while arbitration courts settled questions of pay and conditions. Winlaton forgemen were politically aware and sometimes militant: in 1831 hundreds of them marched on Durham to prevent the Marquis of Londonderry from breaking up a Reform Bill demonstration with his yeomanry, and during Chartist activity ten years later they were rumoured to be mass-producing pikes for the protestors.

Rivals of Crowley's men were those from Hawks of Gateshead which became the biggest ironworks in the North. Hawks' workers were legends in their own lifetime, and the account of their exploits at the Battle of Waterloo passed into comic legend. Wellington tells Ned White of Hawks to take 24 men and shift 400 French soldiers off the top of a hill:

"Just as we turned the corner at the foot of the hill, whee should we meet but Bonipart hees-sel on a lily-white horse, wi' a cocked hat on. 'Where are ye off te , Ned?' says he. 'Wey, te shift yon Frenchmen off yon hill.' 'Whaat!' he says; 'wey, that's maa crack regiment,' he says. 'Nivor mind it,' Aa says; 'Wellington says we hev to shift them, and shifted they'll be noo!' 'Get away man, ye're coddin'' says he. 'Ne coddin' aboot it,' Aa says; 'Cum by!' 'Haud on theen,' he says; an he gallops reet up the hill on his lily-white horse, an' shoots oot, 'Gan back, ma lads, gan back! Heor's Ned White frae Hawks an' fourteen of his cheps comin' up te shift ye. Ye havven't a happorth of chance!'"

Whether it was something in the air or the waters of Derwent and Tyne, this whole area of North-west Durham has a history of protest, and the colliery village of Chopwell just up the Derwent became known in the nineteen-twenties as 'Little Moscow', its Mineworkers Union banner bearing the portraits of Marx and Lenin as well as the more moderate home-grown Keir Hardie.

In the early years of our railway system the cross-country line to Carlisle did not start at Newcastle, but away over the river at Redheugh, opened in 1838. Later they set the line over the river between Scotswood and Blaydon and connected with the newly-built Central Station in the city. For many years there were lines running parallel on both sides of the Tyne between Blaydon and Wylam, but the northern line through Elswick eventually closed and the southern bank through Dunston and Gateshead was preferred.

En route today it serves the huge out-of-town shopping complex known as the Metro Centre, surely one of the rare examples in recent years of railway adaptation rather than closure.

The Metro Centre covers 100 acres of old industrial wasteland. It's the largest of its kind in the country and reckoned no friend at all by the older-established shops and markets in town. It has its own coach-parks and railway station, which also links with the Tyneside Metro system.

Metro Centre, exterior

Chapter Eight

North Bank above Newcastle

Newburn — favourite crossing-place for the Scots before the bridge

The northern bank of the river, which we left appropriately at George Stephenson's trackside cottage by Wylam, is almost a mirror image now of the south side.

There were early collieries around Throckley and Walbottle near where Hadrian's Wall sweeps down to join the Tyne. At Newburn, opposite Ryton, and linked to it by a narrow bridge, there was a ford, the nearest to the sea.

It was this ford which gave Newburn its place in history, for it was used by King David of Scotland in 1346 on his way to ultimate defeat at the Battle of Neville's Cross just outside Durham. Almost exactly 300 years later another Scottish army, of Covenanters this time, used it

Newburn Church — who fired the cannon?

on its way to take Newcastle in the so-called Bishops' War of 1640. Perhaps the hearts of the English defenders were not fully in the struggle, for many of them sympathised with the Puritan Scots, but they were in any case outnumbered over six to one and their earthworks on the Durham bank of the Tyne were outflanked after an intensive softening-up by cannon mounted in Newburn church tower. The Scots then were able to take the town from the South with little opposition.

The church whose tower provided such a convenient artillery platform is yet another in the chain of early places of worship strung along these middle reaches of Tyne. The tower is rather more Norman than pure Saxon, and there is more Norman work in the north aisle. It was in St Michael and all Angels that George Stephenson was first married, in 1802. He repeated the performance eighteen years later with his second wife; son Robert attending as a witness. It was at night-school at Newburn that the older inventor learnt many of his skills.

Far more conspicuous these days than the church tower is the huge brick cone of the old General Electric Company's glassworks, reckoned, at least when it was built, to be the largest in the world. One hundred and twenty feet high, with one-and-three-quarter-million bricks. Today the cone is still a considerable landmark, and has been preserved, perhaps not quite appropriately, as a showroom for four-wheeled-drive vehicles. But the space at the bottom of the cone itself is open to the public, even if they aren't after buying a Land Rover, and houses sculpture and paintings exhibitions. Between it and the river, where once was the celebrated Lemington Gut, is a residential caravan site, or, in modern parlance, a park for mobile homes.

But all this is more accurately in Lemington, which is getting very close to the Scotswood end of Newcastle itself. It was the site of the first integrated ironworks in the North-east, with coke ovens, blast furnaces, rolling-mills, foundry and wrought-iron plant. It was closed down in 1876, by which time the whole area had changed again.

This is also traditionally the upper limit of river navigation at the Hedwin Streams, where annually the mayor of Newcastle and

Glassworks cone at Lemington — once the biggest in the world

other civic bigwigs sailed up and down the river to proclaim their rights — a sort of watery beating of bounds. Lemington was also the finishing line for many of the rowing races which were as much a popular passion in the nineteenth century as football matches today. Tyne oarsmen, mostly river-workers of one sort or another, regularly took on the best from the Thames and from America, and as often as not beat them.

They also produced world champions like 'Honest Bob' Chambers, for whose funeral in 1868 one of the biggest crowds ever on Tyneside turned out. Oarsmen often strained their hearts early in life, but they got heroic send-offs. Today rowers in their sculls, fours and eights, still practice on the quiet reach below Lemington, although the sport has no longer any great popular following.

Rowing used to be Tyneside's most popular sport

Chapter Nine

Scotswood and Armstrong

The river by Scotswood

Now we are getting close to Newcastle itself, looking downstream beyond the bridges at Blaydon, site of the old Chain Bridge at the end of Scotswood Road and now -of the modern A1 Ring Road motor bridge, fast link between Durham and the Far North. For over a century- and-a-half, until less than twenty years ago, the scene to the east of Bells Close and the Scotswood Bridge was one of practically unrelieved heavy industry and the accompanying homes of its workers. For nearly three miles, right along between the Tyne and Scotswood

Road, stood the mighty Elswick Works of Vickers Armstrong, at one time the biggest, most inventive armaments works in the world. For over six generations of workers' lives Armstrongs was Newcastle.

William George Armstrong was the son of a corn merchant operating around the Cowgate, outside Newcastle. Born in 1810, he showed an early interest in ballistics; the story going that he liked smashing people's windows with bits of clay pipe fired from his catapult while at school at Barnard Castle. He started his working life as a solicitor, but his interest in engines, and particularly hydraulics, started him inventing.

In 1845 he sold the idea of applying water pressure from the street pipes in the lower part of Newcastle to drive cranes on an increasingly busy Quayside. Young Armstrong never looked back. In 1847, with a group of local businessmen, he bought a couple of riverside meadows by the then pretty village of Elswick. Here he built a factory and in that he built his cranes. But his interests were to spread rapidly.

Armstrong was what would now be known as a workaholic. He would start at six-thirty each morning alongside his men and was apparently well thought-of by them: one of those rare bosses not afraid to roll up sleeves and have a go himself. His factory would build anything mechanical—moving bridges, railway engines, pumps, ships and guns. Especially guns. Armstrong designed a light field gun with a rifled barrel which fired shells instead of cannon balls. It was too late for the Crimean War, but came in handy for the Indian Mutiny. Armstrong gave

his patents to the Government, thus ensuring himself a knighthood and a lot more orders. Later he sold to any government with cash to spend, and the Armstrong Gun was used by both sides in the American Civil War. He used to test it in Newcastle's pretty Jesmond Dene and up on the fells of Allendale above the South Tyne.

And Armstrong kept expanding. He made mines, armoured plate, shells and later on his firm built tanks, locomotives, aeroplanes, and anything of metal that would sell. As early as 1884 he started a huge shipyard on the river behind his works for the building exclusively of warships. Amalgamations followed, and when William George (now Lord) Armstrong died in 1900 his Elswick Works employed 25,000 men, the biggest concern in Newcastle if not on the Tyne. Later, through takeover, it became Vickers-Armstrong, later simply Vickers.

But it was not just the factories which Armstrong left behind him. He had transformed the face of West Newcastle. Now his works ran for over two miles up to Scotswood, and the steep hill above them became a series of parallel streets crossing Westmorland-road right up to Westgate-road and looking cross-river to Dunston Power Station.

Down on the Scotswood road there were shops , with a pub on almost every corner-end, forty-four of them altogether, and most named after some aspect of work at the factory opposite. There was the Ordnance Arms, the Hydraulic Crane, the Vulcan, the Forge Hammer, etc., etc. It used to be an ambition, a rarely-realised bet among drinkers, to have a gill in every Elswick pub and remain upright. A gill is not a proper gill on

Vickers — the end of an industrial empire

Tyneside but their name for a half-pint, so a pint in each would have been a virtual impossibility, even for the thirsty forge-men from Armstrongs. His Lordship no doubt disapproved, but he did build a school. It numbered its pupils in thousands at a time and was at one time the largest in Newcastle.

It must have seemed in those days to an Armstrong tradesman, and perhaps even more to his wife, that this world of Elswick could never end. Yet it really lasted only a little over a century. Although at one time to have been apprenticed or even just employed at Armstrongs was a ticket to work anywhere in the world of engineering,

amalgamation and recessions diminished the work, the city planners demolished most of the steep old streets (and most of the pubs) and did not always replace them with better accommodation. The Noble-street flats of the 1950s were notoriously badly-planned, and mercifully short-lived.

Now there are factory units and multi-storeyed blocks of flats which could be anywhere in Britain, although they have a spectacular display of daffodils before them in the Spring. Over the Scotswood Road between it and the river is a string of light industry and (sign of the 'nineties times) the Tyneside Business Park, an estate of rather up-market offices where the tanks and guns used to be midwived and nurtured.

I have told the story of the rise and fall of Armstrongs at some length, but must warn now that it will not be possible to deal in such detail with all of the other great industrial names along this river of enterprise.

Hawthorn Leslies, Clarke Chapmans, Palmers of Jarrow and Hebburn, Smith's Docks of St Peter's and North Shields, Holmes' and Reyrolles — all played their part.

Joseph Swan invented the incandescent lamp, and Lord Armstrong lit his country mansion at Cragside, Rothbury with it, the first in the world. Even Andrews Liver and Eno's Fruit salts were invented in Newcastle, with the Co-op's celebrated Pelaw boot polish born just a few miles down-river.

Some of those involved in the development of modern industry may deplore my having gone rather too deeply into the story of enterprises now dead while ignoring their own undoubted achievements. I can only plead that while these may be exciting to those taking part in them, the manufacture of cybernetic gubbins and microchipery is nowhere near as interesting to the rest of us. In the same way that the story and look of ancient buildings like Hexham Abbey are more attractive than the design of a twelve-storey block of modern flats or offices, so it is with industry.

For me anyway, and I'm doing the telling. Computers may turn water into wine and transmute base metals into gold, but the process is not exciting to watch and probably quite impossible to explain. To use a deplorable modern phrase, it is just not sexy.

Chapter Ten

Newcastle, Gateshead and their bridges

New riverside walk below Scotswood Road

So, back to old Newcastle. For well over a century the riverside at Elswick would have been closed, prohibited to non-Armstrong workers. Now there is a continuous footpath all the way from Scotswood to the city centre. It may look pretty dead now compared with the busy old days, but at least you can take the dog for a walk and tell it how full the river used to be. It won't be your fault if it doesn't believe you.

The walkway now is smartly tiled, there are beds of flowers, or at least bushes, which are more

Newcastle — biggest concentration of bridges in Britain

durable, and dog-friendly. There are seats and bits of sculpture and a display board telling the Armstrong story with particular reference to the arched projectile shop, part of which has been preserved for visitors to look at. And of course you can stare across to the Gateshead side where streets even steeper than the Elswick terraces used to heave themselves up the slopes below Bensham-road and Askew-road (Gateshead's answer to the famous thoroughfare to Scotswood)). Some of those terraces had hand-rails, and one or two even big metal staples to help old horses haul their loads. All gone now, part of a lost world since the Sixties, yet I know I didn't imagine it. Today this area is part of Gateshead's main road system, with blocks of high-rise flats above the busy traffic. Apart from the view it could be Wolverhampton.

But next we are in a world of bridges. Running from west to east we have the Blaydon road bridge, the Scotswood ditto, the Redheugh Bridge linking Gateshead's Bensham and Newcastle's Scotswood roads; the King Edward Bridge for the railway (1906), the Queen Elizabeth II also known as the Metro Bridge, carrying the Metro railway link; further downstream Robert Stephenson's masterpiece, the double-decked, cast and wrought iron High Level carrying railway on top and road and pedestrians underneath.

Below this another of Lord Armstrong's creations, the ingenious, hydraulically-powered Swing Bridge, built in 1876 and still opening and closing to let through a diminishing river traffic. It stands on the site of the only crossing Newcastle had for nearly 2,000 years, that built by Hadrian and its medieval successors, one of which was destroyed like most others up-river by the great flood of 1771, when several of the shops built on the bridge were swept away.

And then of course there's the famous Tyne Bridge, the King George V, although it's rarely called that. Some believe it was built as a rehearsal for the Sydney Harbour giant, but there are differences quite apart from sheer size. The Newcastle-Gateshead crossing is slung 100 feet above the river from a great metal bow, its piers deeply anchored at either end. It joins the foot

Swing bridge in foreground — Armstrong-built and still going strong

The Millennium Bridge — busy blinking

of Pilgrim-street — or what is left of that ancient road since they built the huge roundabout in its place — to the Gateshead Highway above the High-street, and it has become the symbol of urban Tyneside, captured on a million films, photographs and videos.

And now there's yet another bridge — as much a wonder in its way as the older symbols of Tyneside.

The Millennium Bridge is a pedestrian crossing. Slender and bow-shaped it tilts so as to allow river traffic to pass easily beneath, and because of its shape and function quickly became known as 'the Blinking Eye'.

It was brought up river in 2000 on one of biggest floating cranes in the world, and dropped into position on both river banks first time, in one go. It was opened to the public in September

Newcastle-Gateshead bridges

Baltic Arts Centre, Gateshead

2001, and lived up to ancient local tradition by being on time and by actually working.

It is rather more than just a bridge, however cunningly made, being the centre of a hugely ambitious redevelopment of Gateshead Quays costing £250 millions and one of the main aspects of the joint approach by Newcastle and Gatehead to become European City of Culture in 2008.

After the Tyne Bridges you have over six miles to travel before you can cross the river dry-shod, and that will be under the water by the tunnels between Howdon and Jarrow.

This district of bridge concentration, surely the biggest in Britain, was historically the oldest, busiest part of the city. This is not the place to go too deeply into its long and colourful past, but you can walk this stretch, from the bottom

The old city walls at Blackfriars

of Forth Banks to the Close behind the Central Station, right along to the Ouseburn under Byker Bridge in the East End, and feel much of the story of the city above and beyond you. They've called this walk Hadrian's Way, and it's appropriate because Hadrian gave his name to what next became Monkchester, then Newcastle. *Pons Aelius* it was to start with, after the Emperor's full name, Publius Aelius Hadrianus, of Spanish extraction.

Newcastle has been a fortress for hundreds of years: in the town itself Hadrian's Wall took in a big fort which stood more or less between the Castle and the Moot Hall today. The Wall itself has been gradually converging on the river from west to east, and stretches are still visible alongside the A69 by the suburb of Benwell, which the Romans called *Condercum*. Then the Normans used the Roman fort site above the river for their castle, first of wood but later strong with

The Guildhall, Sandhill

Bessie Surtees House, Sandhill.

stone. Then in the thirteenth century it was decided to ring the whole town which had grown up around the castle with a continuous wall up to thirty feet high, pierced with six strong gates, and strung out with seventeen towers. It was two miles in extent, even ran along the river frontage, and doubtless included stones from the previous Roman Wall.

The historian Leland in 1540 reckoned that for strength and magnificence it surpassed all city walls in England and most of Europe. The Geordies are Britain's Texans — they like being told they are tops. Although they are not always invulnerable.

In 1644 a Scottish army under Alexander Leslie, Earl of Leven, in support of the Parliamentary forces, took Newcastle, which was for King Charles. This was no easy victory like the Covenanters' four years earlier, when Leslie more or less walked in after his crossing at

John Wesley preached on the Quayside — and they're still at it

Newburn. Newcastle was much better organised in the Civil War, and it took a ten-week siege before the walls were mined and breached, and the mayor and his last-ditch party surrendered from refuge in the Castle keep.

The same walls discouraged the Jacobites in 1715 when Newcastle supported King George, and they were not challenged in the second rising thirty years after, although there was much preparation for attack. Edinburgh had fallen to the rebels and Newcastle was full of troops. The walls were repaired, and all but three of the gates walled up. As the Jacobites under Bonnie Prince Charlie marched over the Border to take Carlisle, General Wade used Newcastle as his headquarters before marching his men along Hadrian's Wall to defeat the Jacobites at Preston, and to re-take Carlisle. In the process he knocked down a lot of the wall to make foundations for his military road. He would not have got away with such an act today, but it was considered natural progression at the time. As one soldier wrote:

> If you'd seen but this road before it was made,
> You'd get down on your knees to thank General Wade.

Newcastle was still busy as a military staging-post before and after Culloden, and in July 1746, after the battle, the Duke of Cumberland, King George's own son and 'Butcher' Cumberland to his enemies, was given the freedom of the city. He had passed through before Culloden, when he was welcomed by '*a kind of illumination*', as the old record puts it, '*the mob having set a popish chapel on fire*'. Now, with victory won,

the city fathers showed '*a token of their high esteem for his many princely virtues, and the grateful sense they entertained of his distinguished services in defence of the laws and liberties of Great Britain.*' There was really nothing new in a royal visit: Newcastle had seen practically every monarch since the Saxon kings, far more than any place outside London.

After the rising the walls were reckoned no longer needed, and they gradually fell, or were pulled, to bits. Most of the towers and gates survived however, at least for a while, being adopted as headquarters by some of the medieval trade guilds of the town—the plumbers, the barber-surgeons and suchlike.

Today rather little remains, and many of the stretches which were preserved until recently, more by luck than judgement, are hedged in with more recent buildings. But it is possible to walk round the city, linking the bits of wall and the towers, and get an idea of old Newcastle that no motorist or shopper can hope for. One of the most impressive sections is that behind the Central Station and high above the river, which until recently formed part of the original Northern Clubs Federation Brewery ('The Fed'). Below it is what is left of a quarter of huge old bonded warehouses which extended along the Close, along with some fine old merchants' houses, up to the Swing Bridge by the Guildhall. The 'Fed' moved over the river to Dunston.

The space in front of the venerable Guildhall (built, as the Maison de Dieu, in 1412, extended in Gothic style 1655, and rebuilt 1823) was called the Sandhill. It was the true heart of old

Newcastle, being the first part a visitor would find on crossing the bridge, and a general gathering-place for the townsfolk *"where were wont to assemble the people for their recreation"* as a proclamation of 1393 put it.

As well as proclamation-readings, all manner of celebrations were held, and still are (on New Year's Eve notably), riots were begun, speeches made. John Wesley preached from the top of the Guildhall steps and had to be rescued from *'the hot-headed geniuses of Sandgate'* by a fishwife called Mrs Bailes, although on another occasion he talked of the poor people *"ready to tread me underfoot out of pure love and kindness."*

It takes all sorts, even in Newcastle.

Underneath the arches — modern style

Chapter Eleven

The Quayside

Theatre Royal: fine architecture in Newcastle's finest street

It is hard these days to visualise the very dramatic shape that Newcastle must have presented in its earlier years. As well as being built up a steep gorge above the river, over 100 feet high, the north bank was split at right angles by a number of deep ravines down which streams flowed into the Tyne. From west to east these were the Skinner Burn, the Lort Burn (which virtually split the old centre in two) and the Pandon Burn at the Sandgate end. Over the centuries these fissures were bridged and eventually built over — the present High Bridge for example. The elegant Georgian Grey street, one of Britain's finest, continuing even more steeply down

Before Dean and Grey streets were built, up from the Sandhill and the bridge-head, winding round the rock of the Norman castle, was the main road into the town — the Great North Road in fact — steep, narrow, and cluttered, but the only route for traffic from the South. This included, in the eighteenth century, the fast stage-coaches which took only thirteen days to get from the English to the Scottish capital via Newcastle "*if God permits*", as the advertisements put it. Later they got the journey to London down to 45 hours, price four guineas, and a later generation boldly flung the main-line railway right across the valley over the old road, right through the castle 100 feet up.

Sandhill and the Side were also the commercial centre: part of the Guildhall was used as the Exchange, and its main business was in coal. Newcastle's coal merchants were not ragged men with black faces bent from years of humping sacks, but extremely wealthy businessmen called the 'Hostmen'. They had a monopoly of the coal trade and lorded it over the whole length of the river to the sea. At the other end of the social scale here were the keelmen, whose job was to convey coal in flat-bottomed barges or 'keels' down river to load the sailing collier-boats near by the mouth; the Tyne until last century being notoriously badly dredged.

These keels were descendants of the old Viking boats, shallow-draughted, oval-shaped, and propelled with the aid of one lug-sail by two oars, one fore and the other aft, which also acted as a rudder. They each held twenty tons of coal and were crewed by two men and a boy who were

Dean Street — railway and cathedral

through Dean-street to the Sandhill follows the line of the now invisible Lort Burn. Once it had even been navigable for a stretch, and Edward I is said to have ordered a galley to be built in a boatyard near the confluence. Today the only hint a visitor might get of any nautical history is in the name 'Painter Heugh' a way up the eastern side of Dean-street.

Dean Street — once the Great North Road

supposed even in Napoleonic times to be exempt from the Press Gang.

Recruited originally from the wild men of the Borders, these keelmen were a tight-knit body, considered themselves a separate community from the rest of the town, and combined in one of the earliest and most effective trade unions in Britain, grimly opposing new methods of coal-loading as well as fighting for wages.

In 1701 they built their own hospital up on the City-road outside the walls above Sandgate. The Bishop of Ely described it:

> "I have heard of many hospitals, the work of rich men; but this was the first I ever saw or heard of which had been built by the poor."

It still stands today, renovated as student accommodation, with a new Salvation Army men's hostel next door.

Sandgate itself, once known as the Wapping of

Keelmen's Hospital

Newcastle, was a mass of narrow lanes running up the hill, but also with some fine waterside houses as well as shipyards, a brewery, and the Ropery Banks which had the first of the port's famous ballast hills, where sea-going ships dumped stone ballast which was then carried on the heads of the women-folk.

These were by all accounts as hard a set of lasses as you would find, and on more than one occasion when their men were in trouble with the law, they turned their aggressive skills rather than their charms on the authorities.

They and their sweethearts figure in many of the best-known songs from Tyneside, from *The Keel Row* itself which was—maybe still is—learnt in schools all over the world, to *The Sandgate Girl's Lamentation:*

> I was a young maid truly,
> And lived in Sandgate Street;
> I thought to marry a good man,
> To keep me warm at neet.
>
> He's an ugly body, a bubbly body,
> An ill-far'd hideous loon;
> For I have married a keelman,
> And my good days are done.

Sandgate was undoubtedly a quarter in its own right, but the whole of the crowded old Quayside was distinctive, its streets running sheer up the Tyne gorge sides in flights of steps known as

Sunday Morning
Quayside Market

True heart
of Newcastle

'chares'. There was the Dark Chare, the Blew Anker Chare, Pepper Corn Chare, Grundon Chare and chares named after souls long since gone and forgotten — Palester Chare, Hornsby's Chare, Colvin's Chare and so on. Most of these tight and doubtless quite insanitary stair-streets were destroyed in the Great Fire of 1854.

Every historical city should have had its Great Fire, and Newcastle certainly had its. In fact it caught it from Gateshead where, in the middle of an October night, a textiles factory caught fire and spread its flames swiftly to a chemical works alongside.

Once that was burning well and exploding in a most colourful fashion, the fire only needed a good stiff breeze to travel via the rigging of the ships packed in the crowded river over to the opposite shore, where the warren of narrow streets stood little chance.

A total of 53 people were killed, many more badly injured, and over 800 families made homeless. Public subscription nation-wide raised £11,000 for the victims, but a longer-term benefit was to the city itself: the fire had cleared away some of its worst slums and a newer, better-built Quayside emerged from the ashes.

This riverside area had been changing for a while. First came the High Level Bridge in 1849, then Armstrong's Swing Bridge in 1876, and then the mighty Tyne Bridge in 1928. Much old property had to be cleared to make room for each of them. But what might be called the old Quayside spirit never died.

From way back it had been a place for public activity, and its street markets were always popular. At times of celebration public water taps were filled with wine or beer and presumably the strongest drinkers got the most. Or the roughest. When George IV was crowned in 1821 Sandhill Pant *presented an almost indescribable scene of uproarious confusion*. People fought to get to the booze whilst others *"having made too free with the rosy god, fell to the ground, a height of nine feet, one of them being severely hurt."*

And now, in spite of the fact that Newcastle Riverside in common with dock areas in London, Liverpool and Bristol has been gentrified, and is now extremely fashionable, not to say expensive, to live, wine or dine in, the old Sunday-morning market still flourishes, with stallholders from all over the North shouting their wares and blocking off the streets to traffic. The true and ancient heart of Newcastle beats again.

The new Law Courts are back on the Quay today. They used to hold the Assizes in the Guildhall in a cramped old court-room with spiked docks still hung with iron manacles under a hammer-beam ceiling. Now the Crown Court is probably the grandest building on the river-front—surely another sign of the times.

New Law Courts — pride of place on Quayside

136

Chapter Twelve

Byker and the Ouseburn

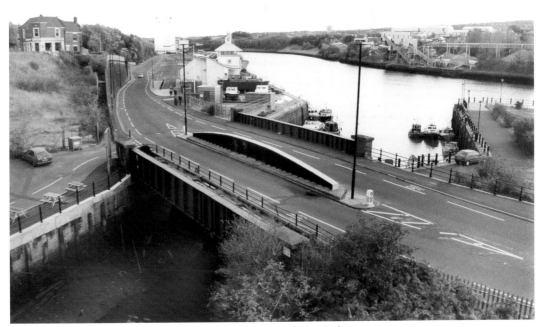

Mouth of the Ouseburn, Byker

What to say about the comparable stretch of waterfront over in Gateshead? Historically rather little, since it was always overshadowed by Newcastle. It has, though, one building whose history matches its neighbour's — the Church of St Mary at the top of the bank where the Tyne Bridge leaves the town. Here in 1080, the new Norman rule becoming increasingly unpopular, the crowd called out and butchered the French Bishop Walcher, setting fire to the church and killing his guard. Afterwards they marched on Durham where they failed to take the castle. Now

Walcher was an important man in the new occupation's hierarchy. He had bought the earldom of Northumberland and now William sent his own brother Odo, Bishop of Bayeux and likewise more a Norman warrior than a priest of peace, being at the same time Earl of Kent, to take revenge. Odo put many to death and reduced the country round the Tyne to a wasteland.

St Mary's Church was rebuilt, rather higher up than the original, and its latest version stands, overshadowed by a large modern office-block, but looking straight across the river to All Saints in Newcastle, the fine semi-circular Renaissance-style building which replaced an older church in 1786, right above the teeming Quayside slum. It is supposed to have been built on the site of a Roman pantheon—a temple to all the gods—and hence the name Pandon for the dene which ran below it. But who knows? All Saints was deconsecrated in 1961 and converted into offices and a lecture-theatre for schoolchildren.

At the time of Newcastle's greatest mercantile prosperity, in the eighteenth and nineteenth centuries, there were a number of riverside wharves whose names

All Saints Church

give an indication of the extent of Tyne trade. There was a London Wharf, and likewise Hamburg and Rotterdam Wharves. These were all levelled when the Quayside was extended up to the Ouseburn below Byker.

Trinity House

Still intact, though, on the Broad Chare below All Saints, is the fine Trinity House, started in the fourteenth century by the Fellowship of Masters and Mariners of Ships of the Town of Newcastle upon Tyne, as a chapel, alms house and meeting-place. It is a charming old building with courtyards and a banqueting-hall. Trinity House was responsible for coastal navigation and later for the upkeep of lighthouses.

It is hard now to envisage the amount of industry which went on round here until about 100 years ago. There were little shipyards, there were coal-staiths (in spite of the keelmen's opposition), and there was a two-and-a-half-mile tunnel to haul coals underground all the way from the colliery at Spital Tongues to the north of Newcastle right down to the river and the keels. But above all here there was glass. Its manufacture was the second most important industry on the river to coal, started largely by Huguenot refugees from Lorraine, and at one time it was said to supply the whole of the kingdom with window-glass. The Ouseburn still has a Glasshouse Bridge at its river end.

The name 'Ouseburn' may sound appropriate to its generally run-down look (though it is much tidier today than it used to be), but R. J.Charleton in his *History of Newcastle-on-Tyne*, 1885, says it was originally called the Ewes Burn and was indeed a pretty, pastoral sort of place, the stream trickling down from Heaton and Jesmond

> "and most part of its valley is for beautiful scenery not surpassed in England."

A little above the river, by the old Ropery Banks, there was an area which became known as 'Egypt' on account of its extensive granaries. Today on City-road are the studios of Tyne Tees Television and next door one of its workers' handiest watering-holes, the Egypt Cottage. A

Byker bridges span the lower Ouseburn

strange name for a pub until you remember its antecedents.

Byker itself is an old village, and once belonged to one Nicholas de Bikar in the thirteenth century.

It has long been a matter of some working-class pride to say that you come from Byker (almost on a par with belonging to Scotswood-road on the west), and not a few claimed it when they really originated from Heaton to the north of Shields-road, which is not the same thing at all. Byker was, like most of this part of the world,

for some hundreds of years a coal-mining area, as the old song went:

> Byker Hill and Walker Shore—
> Collier lads for evermore!

But there was more to it than coal. There was salmon-fishing in the river—indeed salmon was so plentiful before the real industrial revolution fouled the waters that the apprentices of Newcastle used to have it written into their indentures that their masters should not feed them salmon more than twice a week. At Dent's

Road, Metro and Rail bridges span the Ouseburn Valley

Hole, east of Byker, whaling ships back from the long Greenland voyage used to tie up, and there was in 1751 a public subscription opened for the fitting-out of a regular whaling fleet from the Tyne.

Byker may have been a poor and ugly place, but life there would never have been dull. There was rivalry between the surrounding manors of St Anthony's, St Lawrence's and St Peter's. Today they all merge into each other, but Byker is still Byker, famous now for its mighty bridges which fly across the Ouseburn canyon en route for Shields, and once much favoured by suicides, and the nearby Byker Wall, a highly-progressive housing scheme. Those and the popular children's television soap *Byker Grove* have made the old name famously successful throughout Britain. Old Nicholas de Bikar might be proud.

But as far as the riverside itself today is concerned, there was until recently little to differentiate one mile from another, or, apart

St. Peter's Marina — the old keelmen would never recognise it

from the international-standard athletics stadium at Gateshead, north bank from south. Each side had a similar history — miles of ballast hills where rocks and soil from all corners of the globe were dumped to make way for cargoes outward bound, and mile upon mile of factories which once made everything from boot polish to the innards of ocean liners.

But today the old river-workers of Byker and Walker would hardly recognise their old stamping-grounds. New, and I imagine quite expensive housing development lines the river bank. At St Peter's there is a very smart marina, packed with tidy-looking pleasure-boats (at least I imagine they are for pleasure; it is hard to

imagine any of them ploughing the oceans to chase the whale, or even the sprat). There are smart yacht-basin offices, and a plaque on the wall commemorating the official opening by Margaret Thatcher. This tablet really tells it all, and one imagines the ghosts of the keelmen averting their hollow eyes as they float past looking in vain for their old pubs.

Old names poke through here and there. The Ropery, on whose banks the Sandgate Lass of old song sat and thought of her lover, is now a block of flats whose rents she would certainly have been unable to afford, and there's another called The Moorings by St Lawrence's. Hadrian's Way, the riverside footpath, runs past all this to the Wallsend boundary by the Walker Riverside Park. An easier (or complementary) way to view the area would be to take the Metro line which circles out to the coast and back — the first electric railway line in Britain apart from London's Tube.

On the far bank things are mirrored somewhat: new housing, the Gateshead Stadium (which was one in the eye for Newcastle when it was built largely through the drive of Brendan Foster, the long-distance running champion who was born just down the Tyne at Hebburn), a marina at Friar's Goose nearby .

A strange name, Friar's Goose, on a river of odd names. How it got it I shall not attempt to explain, because I don't know, although it is tempting to invent some totally fantastic explanation. But it was the scene in 1832 of a battle between the miners of the colliery there and the police and bailiffs who had arrived to protect a body of cheaply-imported lead miners, and to evict the striking colliers from their homes to make room for them. This was not so much a strike as a lockout designed to break the new miners' union that had been so successfully formed the previous year.

This sort of mass eviction was general in the coalfield that year, but at Friar's Goose things got out of hand. The police were issued with cartridges packed with swan-shot. Richard Fynes, chronicler of the early miners' struggles in Northumberland and Durham, recorded:

"This act of delivering shot to the constables seriously exasperated the miners, and coupled

Athletics-on-Tyne — and not just the Great North Run

with the insolence of those who were busy putting their furniture to the door, and who, not content with bundling their furniture as if it were rubbish, kept calling them cowards, aroused in the breasts of the men a very dangerous spirit."

The magistrate tried to cut his way out through the miners with his cutlass, brickbats were thrown and the constables fired into the crowd. The arrival of a detachment of the Queen's Bays, accompanied by the Mayor of Newcastle and the

Rector of Gateshead, calmed things down a bit, but forty people, including three women, were arrested and afterwards tried at Durham Assizes. The miners' union was eventually crushed, not to resurrect for a dozen years.

Today the grave of Thomas Hepburn, the self-taught coal-hewer who had led them, can be found in the church yard at Heworth, not far away, well-tended now after being practically forgotten for nearly a century, and the scene now every year of a commemoration by what is left of a later, more powerful union whose members nevertheless experienced trouble on a scale comparable to that of their predecessors.

"Shorter Hours and Better Education for Miners" it reads now over the top of Hepburn's grave-stone. Ironically perhaps, a century after his death he was celebrated nationally on a British postage stamp. A once-forgotten working-class hero remembered. At last.

The Thomas Hepburn Commemoration Service at the graveside, Heworth Church (2003)

Chapter Thirteen

Wallsend and Howdon

Segedunum, Wallsend — for years Wallsend's Roman past was hidden beneath Swan Hunters;
now the two have grown side by side

Next stop on the northern bank is Wallsend, which the Romans called Segedunum. Here, literally, their mighty wall ended, or began, depending on which way they were heading.

It was built on a ninety-degree bend in the river. One way you could see upstream to Felling, four miles away on the Durham bank: the other even further down to Jarrow Slake within smell of the sea.

Segedunum housed at one time the Fourth Cohort of Lingones, whoever they were, and at another the Second Cohort of Nervians, who presumably were the tribe Shakespeare's Mark Antony mentions Caesar overcoming.

Segedunum is yet another example of Tyneside rediscovering its heritage. A little late perhaps, but better late than never. For years the fort was practically buried under the great shipyard of Swan Hunters, but now, in time for the turn of the millennium, it has been given the full face-lifting works, with its walls properly excavated, a museum, and a viewing tower 150 feet high with Swan's yard looming beside it, modern cheek by Roman jowl.

Swans was the biggest shipbuilder on the Tyne, and it was in their yard here, as the locals will still tell you, that the liner Mauretania was built in 1907. She broke the transatlantic speed records and covered some two million nautical miles before she was broken up.

Swan's record was tremendous: 55 warships in the First World War and 125 in the Second, including the battleship Anson. Wallsend was also the home of Parsons Marine Turbine Company, formed after young Charles Parsons attached a steam turbine to a tiny vessel, named it Turbinia, and took it down himself to Queen Victoria's Diamond Jubilee Spithead Review in 1897. He sailed fast rings round all the warships, an act impossible to imagine happening today. Admiralty orders followed, and Parsons was made.

But before ships Wallsend was famous — surprise, surprise — for its coal. Wallsend household coal was famous all over the kingdom, its name a by-word in domestic heating which

even Dickens mentioned. "We will take him, by twilight, enlivened with a glow of Wallsend." *Lawers Lightwood and Wrayburn in conversation, Our Mutual Friend, Chapter twelve.*

Wallsend Colliery was sunk in 1781, and was the scene of a terrible explosion forty years later which killed 59 men and boys. These were not its first casualties: 22 in seven separate accidents in its first nine years, and a further 102 were to die in just one incident in 1835. The Tsar Nicholas I was reported, when invited underground at Wallsend, to have said:

> "Ah my God, it is the mouth of hell; none but a madman would venture into it!"

Perhaps he was right.

Wallsend coal lasted, though, in a colliery later known as the Rising Sun. Its shafts were further to the north of Wallsend than the old ones had been, and it was not closed until 1969. Its site is now another country park.

Two famous men claimed Wallsend as their birthplace — Robert Stephenson the engineer and bridge-builder, and William Stead the great campaigning editor of Victorian times.

Further downstream where the coast-bound railway line (the Metro) makes a huge leap over the ravine at Willington by a great seven-arch viaduct, kids could once look down from the train to the long roofs of Hood Haggie's Ropeworks and imagine themselves airborne. Not any longer. The ropeworks have changed hands, and the part below the viaduct has been demolished.

Swan-Hunters Yard, Wallsend

Hood Haggies, I remember, had a large female staff. The girls used to go by the name of Haggie's Angels, for no reason that anyone knew although some had sweet enough faces.

The Tyne's north bank was traditionally linked to the Durham side by ferry hereabouts, there being no bridge this side of Newcastle's giants nearly seven miles away, but in 1951 a tunnel was sunk for cyclists and pedestrians, to be followed in 1970 by the present vehicular toll tunnel. The £1 car toll may not be hideously expensive as such prices go these days, but it would be a lot dearer than they used to charge on the ferry between Howdon, east of Wallsend, and Jarrow. It was quite a lively vessel if the old song is anything to go by:

> O, ye taak aboot travels an' voyages far,
> But theor's few beats the trip fre the toon to the Bar.
> As ye gan doon to Tinmuth ye'll heor the chep shoot-
> 'Here's Howdon for Jarrow, ma hinnies loop oot!'

147

Swan-Hunters Yard, Wallsend

There's chemicals, copper, coals, clarts, coke
and stone,
Iron ships, wooden tugs, salt an' sawdust an'
bone,
Manure an' steam ingins, bar-iron an' virr 'ol.
Graunstans an' puddlers (Aa like to be littral).
At Howdon fer Jarrow, Howdon for Jarrow,
Howdon fer Jarrer, ma hinnies, loop oot!

If you stay on the north bank now you enter that part of England which is the first ground these days which greets visitors from Scandinavia, for historically they entered in a far less welcome manner. They call this the Royal Quays now-what used to be the Albert Edward Dock and the Northumberland Dock on either side of Whitehill Point, which had the biggest concentration of railway lines on the river, running down to the old coal staiths.

It is significant that there should have been such a mass of railways just here, for it was in the heyday of Wallsend's coal expansion that the young George Stephenson was appointed engineer at the High Pit of Killingworth Colliery and made his name designing a steam locomotive to haul the coals. The rest, as they say, is history.

Today it is possible for the first time to walk all the way from Wylam, Stephenson's birthplace, along the old waggonway, through Newcastle and Wallsend to the old branch line from Percy

AP Tyne Yard, Wallsend

Main Metro Station here, and catch a steam train along the old wagon route to the steam railway museum two miles or so north where Stephenson's 'Killingworth Billy' is on display.

Back down on the river, the staiths, and the delta-like concentration of mineral lines feeding them with good Northumbrian coal, have gone. Instead the Royal Quays are home to yet another modern phenomenon — the marina. "Welcome to the North-east's most exciting marine village", it says, and there's a floating pub-restaurant called the Earl of Zetland, a rather complex swimming pool called Wet 'n Wild, and a big out-of-town shopping precinct which is not yet as big as Gateshead's Metro monster.

Through this little lot and you're in North Shields, but were going to dodge back now to see what happens if you take the Tyne Tunnel to the other side.

The Earl of Zetland — floating pub-restaurant

Chapter Fourteen

Jarrow — the World of Bede

Jarrow's latest Vikings

Jarrow. Or 'Dorty Jarrer' as they sometimes love to call it, but only among themselves. A town whose name rings forever whenever political protest is mentioned: *The Town That Was Murdered*, as its one-time MP, the fiery little red-headed Ellen Wilkinson called it in her book. It is famous for a lot more in fact, and one aspect of fame leads to another in Jarrow. The story of Charles Mark Palmer was an industrial success story almost as great as Armstrong's.

After inventing the first screw-driven iron collier in 1852, which cut the Tyne-Thames trip down from a month to under a week, Palmer expanded into iron warships, rolling his own armour-plate in Jarrow and developing a huge industrial complex there—blast furnaces, rolling-mills, a slipway and graving-dock. Besides warships Palmers built the first-ever oil tanker. But by 1935 the whole lot was closed down. "*Jarrow must work out its own salvation*" were the notorious words of the then President of the Board of Trade, Viscount Runciman, and so Jarrow tried to.

In 1936 its unemployed marched to London in a carefully organised demonstration. All shades of political opinion were involved and the organisers were to insist that it was to be called a Crusade, not a hunger-march. Understandably perhaps, a lot of Jarrow folk today are tired of hearing about it. They are trying to live down their past, they say, and to look to the future. So although they now have a pub called The Crusader, the statue in the shopping centre shows not a man marching with a banner or sitting on a park bench whistling at nothing, but a brace of stout Viking warriors. Which gives a sort of symbolism, for the Norsemen in their own sweet way, were trying to move towards a better future for themselves and their children. Anyway, the Vikings were undoubtedly in Jarrow—real ones. The broad expanse of Jarrow Slake (as the geographers call it) or Slack (as the locals do) would have given them a grand sheltered harbour well up the river as a good jumping-off point for further exploration or pillage, whichever theory you favour.

And there were pickings to be had right here. The invaders must have known from experience that religious bodies usually chose the best spots to set up their community-homes, and that is what the Saxon monks had done at Jarrow under their leaders Ceolfrid and St Benedict Biscop, who as a younger man had been a disciple of Wilfrid of Hexham and had travelled with him to Rome. Biscop founded a monastery at

Replica Northumbrian Cross at Bede's World

Bede's World

Wearmouth (Sunderland) dedicated to St Peter, and eight years later, in 682, a sister house at Jarrow in the name of St Paul. Its church, a plain, simple affair almost overshadowed now by the electricity pylons round the Slake, is however an established centre of modern pilgrimage. For it was the home for all his adult life of the Venerable Bede, an uneventful-seeming life on the face of it. In his own words:

"I have devoted my energies to the study of the Scriptures, observing monastic discipline and singing the daily services of the Church; study, teaching, and writing have always been my delight."

Yet it was at Jarrow that Bede wrote one of the earliest masterpieces of the English language, his *History of the English Church and People*.

Bede died at Jarrow in 735 A.D., and was buried in the church porch, but afterwards, as the fame of his piety spread, and although he was not formally canonised until 1899, his remains were exhumed and re-buried in the Galilee Chapel of Durham Cathedral, apparently stolen by a Durham monk called Elfred Westoe, who had charge of St Cuthbert's miraculous remains. He first tucked Bede in beside Cuthbert but Bede was re-buried once again after a second exhumation. Bede, incidentally, is the only Englishman mentioned by Dante in the *Divine Comedy*—significantly in the *Paradiso*.

Today the site of Bede's monastery and the Church of St Paul has been renamed, perhaps inevitably the way heritage has lately become a full industry. *'Bede's World'* it's called now, and there are plenty of car and coach parks round about. Now Scandinavians can turn up in more peaceful fashion than was once their custom.

It was fifty years after Bede's death that the Danes made their first raid on the Northumberland coast. They plundered Jarrow, but did not have things all their own way, as they were chased off by the united forces of Northumbria and Mercia, their leader killed, and the remnants of their retreating fleet wrecked on the rocks off Tynemouth. They were more successful a century later under Halfdane, but they left Jarrow standing if a little knocked about.

Jarrow Slake was the scene, in 1832, of a macabre ending to the first big struggle of the miners of the North against the pit-owners. (see page 144) After an initially successful strike the owners retaliated and forced the men back to work. It was a violent dispute: troops were sent to keep order, along with a detachment of the newly-formed Metropolitan Police, and a number of people lost their lives. Among them was one Nicholas Fairless, a magistrate, who, on his way between South Shields and Jarrow, was knocked from his horse and died. A miner called William Jobling who was apparently what today would be termed 'not the full shilling', got the blame and was publicly hanged in Durham Market Place although there were doubts about his guilt. His body was afterwards paraded around the colliery villages as a warning , and finally coated with pitch and hung in a gibbet cage out above the mud of the Slake. Jobling's body disappeared a few days afterwards, and was never found.

Jarrow of course, in common with most settlements on the Tyne, was a coal-mining community as well as a shipbuilding centre. Like Wallsend across the water it had an appalling casualty record. One hundred and thirty-one miners were killed in the thirty years after 1815, including 42 in 1830 and 39 in 1845. It was at the inquiry into the latter (they had at last got around to holding inquests on miners) that a Mr James Mather of South Shields said in support of the men:

> "Deeds have been done in the darkness of the mine, and amidst the most appalling dangers, which ennoble our common nature, and which, if done in the light of day and before the world, would have covered those humble miners with glory. Their deeds are forgotten, and their names only remembered by their sorrowing friends and families."

Perhaps his words should now serve as an epitaph to the whole industry.

Chapter Fifteen

South Shields

South Shields Market Place

And so to South Shields, through its suburbs of Tyne Dock and Laygate. It is country which will be familiar to devotees of the novelist Catherine Cookson: as it tells you, *"You are now entering Cookson Country"*.

She herself described her birthplace at Simonside Place, Tyne Dock, early last century:

"Just a cluster of houses within three minutes walk, under five great slime-dripping arches,

Tyne Dock: Export cars from the Nissan Factory

of the actual dock gates; and yet we were on the verge of what was known as the country."

Today you can find a reconstruction of the street of la Cookson's birth in the South Shields Museum and Art Gallery. You can no longer see the real thing: the street and the slimy arches of Tyne Dock, which for generations carried a wealth of Durham coal to the riverside staiths, are all gone.

But just a few hundred yards downstream, in South Shields itself, very much a town, famous for its coal, its shipbuilding and above all perhaps for having for many years had the biggest proportion per capita of its population working

at sea. It was here that the lifeboat was invented, or evolved; it was here that nearly 2,000 years earlier, the Romans established their entry port to the northern extremities of their empire, and even today, with sea-borne trade heavily declining, it is still unmistakably a sea-port as well as a holiday resort.

Traditionally—that is for most of the past century—South Shields has had a large Muslim population. Most of these, Arabs and Somalis, first came to the town as seamen, but some married local girls and there are now second and even third generation Muslims. The curry-shops of Laygate used to be celebrated long before Indian restaurants became a familiar part of the

British scene, and Shields has had its own mosque for the past forty years.

But the town, like most of our older ports, is changing. The shipyards and marine engineering works have been in decline for some years, and as much of the terrace-housing which was once home to most of the workers has been demolished, so the area around the river-mouth — the Lawe Top and district where the Romans had their fort *Arbeia* — has changed into a more expensive, gentrified area, in line with the Quayside at Newcastle.

The new residents have splendid views—out to sea and over the estuary with their neighbour North Shields strongly evident.

"*South Shields Riverside*", it proclaims on a large board by one new estate, "*A Prestigious Residential, Leisure and Commercial Centre.*" And it looks it. There are clean beaches close by, although ironically the newly-dubbed 'Sand Haven' is part of what used to be the notorious wrecking shore of the Herd Sands. But it's well inside the South Pier now and safe for children and lots of weekend yachtspersons.

New development at Lawe Top, South Shields

Sculptures at Sandhaven

Chapter Sixteen

North Shields

Shields ferry; the old 'Jungle' now tamed, in the background

Ferries (but passenger-only these days) still link the twin towns, between which from time immemorial there has been great rivalry.

South Shields is part of South Tyneside Metropolitan Borough, indeed might be called its capital; North Shields was once part of the Borough of Tynemouth, but both are now in North Tyneside. North Shields has a population of 40,000-odd, whereas its southern neighbour has nearly twice as many. Again, North Shields' importance was based on shipbuilding and on coal export, but it was a fishing port as well.

The Fish Quay is still busy, though like most of its kind round our coasts is not as lively as it

High Lights and Low Lights — line them up and you're safe into the river

once was when squads of young Scotswomen followed the herring.

This used to be a rough old sector of a rough old town, the original part along Clive-street between the Ferry Landing and the Fish Quay. If you couldn't get a fight along here, or up the Borough Bank round the corner, you couldn't have been trying, and there were always plenty of young and not-so-young ladies ready to oblige in a slightly gentler way without bringing on immediate bankruptcy.

There are still plenty of pubs, although sadly the old Northumberland Arms on the Ferry Landing, more popularly known as The Jungle, has now disappeared, its terrace converted into residential

accommodation—respectable too, which is hardly how the old pub would have been described.

It, incidentally, was where the mayor of Newcastle, Archibald Reed, the same man who was mixed up in the affray at Friar's Goose, took refuge from a different mob.

He had sailed down the river—this was in 1819—to open the navigation after one of the frequent keelmen's strikes of the time, and was lucky to escape with his life. The pub windows and doors were smashed with paving-stones, marines opened fire, a local man was shot dead, and a number of officials injured. The mayor and his retinue managed to escape out of the back and in the end the Sixth Dragoons arrived from Newcastle and quietened things down a bit. But then the 'Jungle' always was a lively kind of pub.

Mayors these days have a much quieter time of it than Archibald Reed, who seems to have been mayor for at least six spells in the early nineteenth century. But there had always been friction between Newcastle and Shields.

Newcastle not only thought it owned the whole river but for most practical purposes it did.

Both North and South Shields had started life as collections of fishermen's huts or 'shiels', and there was hell to pay when the Prior of Durham had started a town on the south side and the Prior of Tynemouth much the same on the north, where, according to Newcastle Corporation, "*no town ought to be*". Another grumble was that the Shields fishermen had sold fish "*which ought to be sold at Newcastle, to the great injury of the whole borough, and in detriment of the tolls of Our Lord the King at the Castle.*" The same went for a brewery which the prior had dared to build. This was in 1290, but that state of near-monopoly continued right until 1850 when the Tyne Improvement Commission was set up to share control of the river between its main towns and the Admiralty.

The Commission made itself felt straight away, building the two harbour piers out beyond the river mouth and removing much of the danger from the rocks of the Black Middens on the Tynemouth side and the

High and Low lights and North Shields Fish Quay
Tyne piers in backgrond

161

*Carnival time on North Shields
Fish Quay*

Collingwood's Monument. Nelson's second in command has a bigger statue than his boss's.

road in South Shields, but Wouldhave died poor while Greathead got a parliamentary grant of £1,200, a Trinity House award of £100 and a diamond ring from the Russian Tsar. But life's sometimes like that.

Back to North Shields where a little old pub called the Low Lights Tavern on the Fish Quay marks the presence of one of two towers, old-fashioned lighthouses, which, when lined up, Low and High, indicated a safe ship's passage into the river. By the Low Lights are the remains of Clifford's Fort, built in 1672 as a harbour defence in the Dutch Wars, and improved during the Napoleonic scares. Above it, and strictly in Tynemouth, is the huge monument to Admiral Lord Cuthbert Collingwood, Nelson's Newcastle-born second-in-command at Trafalgar. His figure is 23 feet high, unlikely to be missed by any patriotic mariner sailing into the Tyne.

Herd Sands opposite. Until then hundreds of ships had perished on one or the other and it was after a Newcastle vessel called the *Adventure* got stuck on the latter while hundreds stood on the shore unable to attempt any rescue, that a committee was formed which held a competition for the design of an effective lifeboat. The prize was won by Henry Greathead of South Shields, though some said it should have gone to William Wouldhave, another local man. Today both men share the monument at the end of Ocean-

Knotts Flats, North Shields — 'Lord Haw-Haw' wanted them for a Nazi HQ

Tynemouth Castle and Priory

North Shields Georgian centre takes some finding, but it's a pleasant surprise

Another landmark was—still is—the big block of Knott's Flats, built in 1939 on the top above the Fish Quay which William Joyce, alias 'Lord Haw-Haw', once boasted on the wartime wireless would provide a handy headquarters for the occupying Germans once they took over the Tyne.

Hitler's *Wehrmacht* is long gone; but the flats are still with us, prominent as ever. As is a sizeable chunk of a North Shields which is rarely recognised except by the locals—the quite elegant quarter of Georgian houses tucked behind the main streets by the railway station.

Although, like its twin sister, and like Newcastle Quay, North Shields has had a recent face-lift and become fashionable as never before (at least since the Georgian heyday), it was Tynemouth which people with pretensions usually claimed to live in, even when they didn't quite: Tynemouth, fiefdom of the Dukes of

Northumberland, with its Norman castle and the neighbouring Priory of SS Mary and Oswin. Together in their early days these two buildings must have been one of the most spectacular sights in the kingdom, surrounded on three sides by steep sea-cliffs, and as often as not a violent sea.

It was not quite invulnerable, though: the Danes sacked it more than once and William Rufus took it after a two-month siege when the Earl of Northumberland, Thomas de Mowbray, rebelled.

King Malcolm of Scotland was buried at Tynemouth, as was St Oswin himself, although both bodies were moved later on. Mowbray had put Tynemouth under the control of St Albans

Abbey instead of Durham, and it remained that way until the Dissolution.

If this was a film and not a book, Tynemouth would be a good, corny place to end it, "as the sun sinks slowly behind its venerable ruins". But it doesn't really, unless you see it from a ship, and I prefer the few lines penned, affectionately I'm sure, by one William Brockie and quoted by Tomlinson in his Guide, but not by today's estate agents:

> Farewell to Shields, the filthiest place
> On old Northumbria's dirty face.
> The coal-hole of the British nation,
> The fag-end of the whole creation.

God bless it.

The Bonga (2003) — the biggest ship on the Tyne for many years

Further Reading

An Account of the Mining District of Alston Moor
Thomas Sopwith

Comprehensive Guide to Northumberland
W.W. Tomlinson

A Description and Historical Account of the Town and County of Newcastle upon Tyne
Eneas Mackenzie

Various Journeys
Alex Wills ('The Vagabond')

The Lanercost Chronicles.

The Art of John Martin
William Feaver

A History of the English Church and People
Bede

Chorographia: or a Survey of Newcastle upon Tyne in 1649
William Grey

Northumberland
Ann Sitwell

Northumbrian Heritage 1912-1937
Stanley Owen

The Border—National Forest Park Guide, 1958
John Walton (ed)

The Buildings of England, Northumberland
Nikolaus Pevsner

The Picture of Newcastle upon Tyne (1807)
John Hodgson

Memoirs
Thomas Bewick

Tyneside Songs and Drolleries
Thomas and George Allan

The Early History of Elswick
Alfred Cochrane

Journal
John Wesley:

A History of Newcastle-on-Tyne
R.J. Charleton

The Miners of Northumberland and Durham
Richard Fynes

The Town that was Murdered
Ellen Wilkinson

Our Kate
Catherine Cookson

Castles of Northumberland
Brian Long

Newcastle upon Tyne, its Growth and Achievement
S. Middlebrook

The History of Newcastle upon Tyne
Henry Bourne

The History and Antiquities of the Town and County of the Town of Newcastle upon Tyne
John Brand

History of Newcastle and Gateshead During the Fourteenth to Seventeenth Centuries
Richard Welford

Local Records
John Sykes

Rise of the British Coal Industry
J.U. Nef

The Middle Marches
G.M. Trevelyan

Waters of Tyne
T.H Rowland

Railways of North East England
K.Hoole